# Jean Cocteau
## Updated Edition

## Twayne's World Authors Series
### French Literature

David O'Connell, Editor
*Georgia State University*

TWAS 84

JEAN COCTEAU
French Embassy Press and Information Division

# *Jean Cocteau*
## *Updated Edition*

## By Bettina L. Knapp

*Hunter College and the Graduate Center*
*of the City University of New York*

Twayne Publishers
*A Division of G. K. Hall & Co.* • *Boston*

*Jean Cocteau, Updated Edition*
Bettina L. Knapp

Copyright 1989 by G. K. Hall & Co.
All rights reserved.
Published by Twayne Publishers
A Division of G. K. Hall & Co.
70 Lincoln Street
Boston, Massachusetts 02111

First edition © 1970, Twayne Publishers, Inc.

Copyediting supervised by Barbara Sutton
Book production by Janet Z. Reynolds
Book design by Barbara Anderson

Typeset in 11 pt. Garamond
by Huron Valley Graphics, Inc., Ann Arbor, Michigan

Printed on permanent/durable acid-free paper
and bound in the United States of America

**Library of Congress Cataloging-in-Publication Data**

Knapp, Bettina Liebowitz, 1926–
  Jean Cocteau / by Bettina L. Knapp.—Updated ed.
    p.   cm.—(Twayne's world authors series ; TWAS 84, French
  literature)
    Bibliography: p.
    Includes index.
    ISBN 0-8057-8239-7 (alk. paper)
    1. Cocteau, Jean, 1889–1963—Criticism and interpretation.
  I. Title.   II. Series: Twayne's world authors series ; TWAS 84.
  III. Series: Twayne's world authors series. French literature.
  PQ2605.015Z689   1989
  848'.91209—dc19                                           88-37316
                                                              CIP

*To Béatrix and Philip Sisson*
*To Sidonia and René Taupin*

# Contents

*About the Author*
*Preface*
*Chronology*

Chapter One
Ends and Beginnings        1

Chapter Two
Scandal . . . Scandal . . .        13

Chapter Three
Retrenchment—A New Reality        34

Chapter Four
Pain Killers        53

Chapter Five
The Struggle        69

Chapter Six
The Holocaust        94

Chapter Seven
A Poet's Solitude        110

*Conclusion*        137
*Notes and References*        143
*Selected Bibliography*        149
*Index*        153

# About the Author

Bettina L. Knapp received her B.A. from Barnard College and her M.A. from Columbia University and has studied at the Sorbonne. She is professor of French and Comparative Literatures at Hunter College and the Graduate Center of the City University of New York. She has received a Guggenheim Fellowship and awards from the American Philosophical Society, the Research Foundation of the City University of New York, and the Shuster Fund. She is a member of PEN and was named officer of the Order of the Palmes Académiques by the French government.

Knapp is the author of numerous works, including *Louis Jouvet, Man of the Theatre; Gérard de Nerval, the Mystic's Dilemma; Antonin Artaud, Man of Vision; A Jungian Approach to Literature; Architecture, Arche-Vision, and the Writer; Women in Twentieth-Century Literature;* and *Music, Archetype, and the Writer.* Also for the Twayne World Authors Series, she has written *Jean Genet* and *Jean Genet, Revised Edition; George Duhamel; Maurice Maeterlinck; Sacha Guitry;* and *Fernand Crommelynck.*

# Preface

Affable, imaginative, a man with unlimited energy—such were the qualities Jean Cocteau displayed when I first met him in New York City in 1949, where he had come to co-direct his play *The Eagle with Two Heads.*

Indeed, Cocteau was striking. He was of slender build. His gray hair framed an intensely expressive face, with thin lips set tightly against fine white teeth, a nose pointed forward into the distance, a large forehead rising gently above deep-set eyes. We shook hands, and Cocteau began speaking almost immediately. He radiated warmth, and his enthusiasm became contagious to the point of infusing me with a strange fervor and fascination.

Cocteau broached many subjects on that wintry afternoon. As he talked, his entire being seemed to be in perpetual motion. In fact, it could even be said that his body acted as the transforming agent for his innermost thoughts. When speaking about the theater, he gesticulated, enacting as he went along certain stances assumed by his various characters: Orpheus, Oedipus, Galahad. His whole frame moved gracefully forth as he mentioned Stravinsky, atonal music, or the ballet. He was less mobile, perhaps more earnest, when he took up the problems of the novel. He derogated sentimental, maudlin, and romantic works with their usual well-made plot lines and forcefully advocated the virtues of objective, controlled, nonpsychological work. As for poetry, he barely moved when alluding to it; it was as if a most profound chord were stirred within him by the very mention of the word. When it came to a discussion of his graphic art, he merely drew out a pen and a large sheet of paper and sketched one of his Greek-like faces for me.

Years later, in 1961, I saw Jean Cocteau again at Villefranche-sur-Mer. He had come to this small port town in the south of France to visit the chapel he had decorated which had been dedicated to Saint Peter by the fishermen of that area right opposite M. Guy Galbois's Hotel Welcome. The seventy-two-year-old Cocteau I now saw was as alive and as scintillating as ever—perhaps even more so.

Jean Cocteau has become a legend. His versatility is attested to by the fact that he successfully wrote poetry, novels, plays, and art criticism. In addition, he was a painter, director, designer, and an extraordinary filmmaker. He was part and parcel of an age he helped to create and which dates back to those exciting days of 1912, when the Russian Ballet was the rage of Paris; it includes the "Esprit Nouveau" era of which Guillaume Apollinaire was the spokesman; the cubism of Picasso and Braque; the jazz age, the Roaring Twenties and the two world wars. Though Cocteau's works are intrinsically rooted in the various eras, they remain, at the same time, aloof from them. They are personal expressions of one man's literary credo. They treat human problems of the most basic kind, and for this reason they stand beyond time. One need only attend a production of *Orpheus* or *The Infernal Machine,* or watch the film *The Blood of a Poet* to appreciate this duality—the brilliant representation of an era and, at the same time, the transcending of it.

Yet Cocteau presents somewhat of a paradox. His very versatility and inventiveness frequently worked to his disadvantage. On occasions, it seemed as if he were seeking to sidestep life, fearful perhaps of what he would find around him and within himself. At these periods he would write voluminously. Some of his works fell far short of being interesting. What accounted for such frenetic activity? Enormously imaginative, talented, and ingenious, Cocteau was a man trying to escape facing up to a painful truth about himself; that he was not a true *creator* in the sense of a Picasso or of a Balzac. He could not, at least on a conscious level, accept this fact. He was forever trying, therefore, to prove, through his literary activities, the contrary of what he knew to be the case. Because Cocteau was fundamentally not a creator, he was always in need of some outside force to set his own "creative" machinery working. The various catalysts in his life (Stravinsky, Diaghilev, Picasso, Radiguet, Maritain, Sartre) succeeded in activating what was most profound within him—that strange substance that lives within the artist—and from this prima materia emerged works in the class of *Thomas the Impostor* and *Children of the Game.* But there were other times, when Cocteau's writings (the play *The Typewriter,* the poem "Léone") were peripheral, skimming surfaces only, and deserved the criticisms of "flippant" and "superficial" that they elicited.

Like Proteus, Cocteau was a many-sided individual and for this reason was difficult to understand. In this volume I try to explicate these complexities, to unravel legend from reality, to analyze Cocteau's personality and his works. I discuss Cocteau's writings from both a literary and psychological point of view in an effort to determine his influences and to point up his originality and worth.

I wish to thank my friends Mrs. Estelle Weinrib for her editorial help and Professor Alba della Fazia Amoia for her wise counsel and perpetual encouragement in the preparation of this manuscript; also Dr. Edward Edinger, Professors René and Sidonia Taupin, Professor and Mrs. Philip R. Sisson, Dr. and Mme Ado Avrane, Mme Denise Macagno, Mr. and Mrs. George Chimes, Professors Maxwell Smith and Sylvia Bowman, and Frank Kirk.

My profoundest thanks go to my husband, Russell S. Knapp, for his positive attitude toward life; to my mother Emily Gresser Liebowitz for her constructive suggestions—and of course to my two sons.

Finally, I wish to thank Hill and Wang for permitting me to quote from *Cocteau: Five Plays,* and New Directions Publishing Company for allowing me to quote from Michael Benedikt's translation of *The Wedding on the Eiffel Tower.*

Bettina L. Knapp

*Hunter College and the*
*Graduate Center of the*
*City University of New York*

# Chronology

1889   Jean Cocteau born 5 July at Maisons-Laffitte (Seine and Oise) into a wealthy bourgeois family.

1899   Jean's father, to whom he was deeply attached, dies. Mme Cocteau moves to Paris with Jean, his brother Paul, and his sister Marthe. Family lives in grandparents' private home, which in time becomes a dazzling magical world for the youngster. Jean begins his studies at the Lycée Condorcet, which he calls a "sinister" experience.

1906   Edouard de Max of the Comédie-Française organizes a public reading of Cocteau's poems at the Théâtre Femina in Paris. Cocteau founds a literary magazine, *Schéhérazade,* with Maurice Rostand and François Bernouard.

1909   Publication of Cocteau's first book of verse, *Aladdin's Lamp (La Lampe d'Aladin).*

1910   Publication of a second book of verse, *The Frivolous Prince (Le Prince frivole).*

1912   Moves to Hotel Biron where Rodin lives. Meets Serge Diaghilev and Igor Stravinsky.

1913   André Gide's stinging criticism of Cocteau's poetry and Diaghilev's statement to him, "Astound me," encourage Cocteau to rethink his "facile" creative output. Goes to Leysen, Switzerland, with Stravinsky. Withdraws from society and writes *The Potomak (Le Potomak),* a fascinating collection of drawings, poems, and prose dialogues.

1914   Volunteers for army but not accepted for medical reasons. Serves illegally as ambulance driver on the Belgian front. Discovered by authorities and discharged. Begins the *Discourse of the Great Sleep (Discours du grand sommeil),* a collection of poems about the horrors of war. Friendship with aviator Roland Garros to whom he dedicates a book of poetry, *The Cape of Good Hope (Le Cap de Bonne-Espérance).*

1916   Begins haunting Montparnasse with Amedeo Modigliani, Guillaume Apollinaire, Max Jacob, Paul Reverdy, André Salmon,

Blaise Cendrars. Meets Pablo Picasso, whom he introduces to Serge Diaghilev.

1917    Scandal follows the performance of the ballet *Parade* at the Chatelet, the argument for which was written by Cocteau, the music by Erik Satie, the sets and costumes by Picasso.

1918    Founds, together with Cendrars, Les Editions de la Sirène where *The Rooster and the Harlequin* (*Le Coq et l'arlequin*) is published. Misunderstanding with Stravinsky.

1919    Meets Raymond Radiguet who becomes his lover. Begins a series of newspaper articles for *Paris-Midi* (11 March–11 August).

1920    The pantomime *The Do-Nothing Bar* (*Le Beouf sur le toit*) performed by the famed clowns, the Fratellini brothers, with masks and sets by Raoul Dufy and music by Darius Milhaud.

1921    The play, *The Wedding on the Eiffel Tower* (*Les Mariés de la Tour Eiffel*) is performed. Writes a critical essay "Professional Secret" ("Le Secret professionnel").

1922    Publication of the novels *The Great Split* (*Le Grand écart*) and *The Impostor* (*Thomas l'Imposteur*) and a book of verse, *Plain-Chant*.

1923    Radiguet dies from typhoid.

1924    Cocteau goes through a period of depression; begins taking opium.

1925    First opium cure suggested by Jacques Maritain and Paul Reverdy (Clinique des Thermes). Sojourns at Villefranche-sur-Mer (Hotel Welcome). Meets Christian Bérard. Writes the poems "Opéra," "The Angel Heurtebise" ("L'Ange Heurtebise"). Correspondence with Jacques Maritain. Finishes the play *Orpheus* (*Orphée*). Reconciliation with Stravinsky. Misunderstanding with the surrealists.

1926    Premiere of the play *Orpheus*, labeled by Cocteau a "meditation upon death." Meets Desbordes.

1928    Prefaces *I Adore* by Desbordes, which scandalizes the Catholic circles. Saint-Cloud Clinic (December 1928–April 1929).

1929    Reads *The Human Voice* for the Comédie-Française's acceptance committee. Writes what has become a classic of its kind, the novel, *The Children of the Game* (*Les Enfants terribles*).

1931    Begins the film *The Blood of a Poet* (*Le Sang d'un poète*). Ill with typhoid.

1932 Finishes the play *The Infernal Machine* (*La Machine infernale*).

1933 Completes the play *The Knights of the Round Table* (*Les Chevaliers de la table ronde*) at the home of Igor Markevitch.

1934 *The Infernal Machine* opens, directed by Louis Jouvet with sets by Christian Bérard. Writes his autobiographical *Portraits-souvenir* for *Figaro*.

1936 Travels around the world in eighty days.

1937 Writes regular column in *Ce Soir* (March 1937–March 1938).

1938 Completes the play *Intimate Relations* (*Les Parents terribles*).

1939 Completes the play *The Holy Terrors* (*Les Monstres sacrés*).

1940 Leaves Paris for Perpignan. Writes the play *The Typewriter* (*La Machine à écrire*).

1941 Moves into Palais Royal, 36 Rue Montpensier. *The Typewriter* and *Intimate Relations* are banned. Writes articles for *Comoedia* entitled "Foyer des artistes." Finishes *Renaud and Armide,* a pastoral play with sets by Christian Bérard and music by Georges Auric. Is beaten on the Champs-Elysées by members of the LVF, a fascist French organization.

1942 Completes the film *The Eternal Return* (*L'Eternel retour*). Testifies in favor of Jean Genet in court.

1945 The film *Beauty and the Beast* (*La Belle et la bête*) premieres.

1946 Writes the play *The Eagle with Two Heads* (*L'Aigle à deux têtes*), the series of essays *The Difficulty of Being* (*La Difficulté d'être*), and the poem "The Crucifixion."

1947 Moves to Milly-la-Forêt (Seine and Oise) and begins his film *Orpheus.*

1948 Designs the Aubusson tapestry "Judith and Holofernes."

1949 Travels to the United States (January). Writes "Letter to Americans" on his return flight. Tours the Mideast with a theatrical company 6–24 March.

1950 Decorates the home of Mme Alec Weisweiller, the Villa Santo Sospir (Saint-Jean-Cap-Ferrat), where he remains as a guest.

1951 Finishes the play *Bacchus.* Breaks with François Mauriac.

1952 Completes a volume of essays *Journal of One Unknown* (*Journal d'un inconnu*).

1953    Writes poems for the collection Clear-Obscure (*Clair-Obscur*). Travels to Spain. Writes "The Corrida of May 1st" describing the bullfight he had witnessed. Suffers a severe heart attack. Remains bedridden for some weeks.

1955    Becomes a member of the Royal Belgian Academy and of the French Academy.

1956    Receives on honorary doctor of letters from Oxford. Paints frescoes at the City Hall in Menton and the Chapel of Saint Peter at Villefranche-sur-Mer.

1963    Dies on 11 October at Milly-la-Forêt.

# Chapter One
# Ends and Beginnings

I hope to be read by people who remain children at all costs. I can ferret them out from among thousands. A glance which looks out upon the pristine magic of the world is better protection from the insults heaped upon us by age, than all the beauty treatments, all the diets. [1]

The name Jean Cocteau evokes an age, dynamic and sizzling; the works, a world of fantasy, mystery, and excitement—a series of ends and beginnings.

* Jean Cocteau was born on 5 July 1889 at Maisons-Laffitte, near Paris, into a wealthy bourgeois family that had a respectable share of stockbrokers and admirals. * His parents, Georges Cocteau and the former Eugénie Lecomte, provided him as a matter of course with substantial economic security and entrées into society. In addition, Jean had natural gifts: he was handsome, slim, with dark hair combed forward to cover a broad forehead, a thin straight nose, and tender but piercing eyes which seemed to shine right into a misty distance. An extrovert who exuded charm, humor, and candor, he captivated those about him.

As a youngster he spent his vacations with his family, which included his brother Paul, his sister Marthe, and his cousins who regularly visited his home on Place Sully in Maisons-Laffitte. There, near the castle designed by the architect Mansart, also responsible for Versailles, the children ran and played. Jean generated an aura of mystery around the glorious gardens surrounding the castle with their lanes, linden trees, and fountains. Another world emerged, transformed by his imagination into a realm of magic and secrecy—available to his child's self only.

Cocteau's favorite place, however, was Paris: "I was born a Parisian, I speak Parisian, my accent is Parisian." When in the city, to which his family moved in 1889, he lived at 45 rue La Bruyère in his grandparent's private home. Although near Pigalle, it was elegant at the time. For him this house too became a fantasy land: a dazzling magical world.

The upper floors of the mansion, occupied by his grandparents for whom he felt genuine affection, seemed filled with intrigue. The silver tube with its gonglike resonant sounds each time water flowed into it, was a source of endless fascination; the books that ornamented the shelves, the Greek busts, drawings by Ingres, a painting by Delacroix, vases from Cyprus, and several Stradivari, provided endlessly enthralling stimuli for fantasies and visions of all sorts. Particularly entrancing was the person of the internationally famous violinist, Sarasate. On those nights when Jean's grandfather, a cellist, invited his friends to play string quartets, the irrepressible children would watch, hidden behind the nearby halberd, as M. Sarasate performed the same automatic gestures each time he arrived. First, he looked into the hall mirror, then he straightened his hair, then entered the salon. Later, as the renowned musician regaled the guests with stories of his various conquests of a professional nature, Jean and the others, filled with admiration and wonder, would crawl up and down the staircase, peering all the while at their grand visitor.

The theater, however, became the truly irresistible land of enchantment for the ten-year-old lad: remote, mysterious, and forbidding. His mother seemed to symbolize the theater with the ritual she enacted on the nights she attended a performance at the Comédie-Française. There was the perfume aimed to intoxicate; the powder whose sole purpose seemed to be the beclouding of reality; the red velvet gown with balloon sleeves and glittering with embroidered black jet, designed to present her beautiful body forcefully; the jewels, the fur coat, and the black-lace fan; and the final dramatic exit on the arm of her husband into the world of glamorous fantasy.

Nourished by an ever dynamic imagination, Cocteau was intrigued by certain names he heard bandied about. From the age of twelve on, he recounts in *Portraits-souvenir,* that he and his friends used to wait outside of the theater to see the famous actress Madame Réjane emerge. Exquisitely intelligent, her subtle portrayals brought crowds rushing to attend her performances in such plays as *Madame Sans-Gêne* by Victorien Sardou. Sarah Bernhardt had also been one of Cocteau's favorites. Indeed, she had already become a myth for all the world. Eccentric, passionate, self-willed, even cruel, she held Paris enthralled as she strode on stage as Phèdre, as Hamlet, and L'Aiglon. But it was perhaps the aging lion of the Comédie-Française, Mounet-Sully, who left the most lasting impression on the young Cocteau. When gouging out his eyes in his unforgettable portrayal of Oedipus, he assumed a sculpturesque quality, roared like a wild animal, bounded forth, his mane shaking in the distance with frenzied pain. And there were so many other "monstres sacrés," idols of Cocteau as well as a whole generation of theatergoers: the "divine" Madame Barthet, the handsome, unconventional, tender Edouard de Max who cut such a fine figure as Nero. Cocteau found music-hall stars equally beguiling: Yvette Guilbert, the *diseuse* with the long black gloves whose naughty songs seduced audiences from one end of the world to the other; the wasp-waist and serpentine Polaire, the dancer "la belle Otéro"; Mistinguett who displayed her charms at the Eldorado in such songs as "J'ai le coeur en feu! feu! feu!"

Circus life also beckoned to the young Cocteau; the extraordinary clowns Footit and Chocolat, immortalized by Toulouse-Lautrec, entertained children and the aged alike with their extraordinary impersonations.

As for the ice palace, it was an ever-exciting place of rendezvous. All the "nice" children, including the young Cocteau, were taken to the palace by their governesses to practice their skating before five o'clock, but they were swept away after the bewitching hour. At that time, the gorgeously gowned *grandes cocottes,* just returning from their ride in the Bois de Boulogne, would make their entrance. It was at the ice palace at the Champs-Élysées that Cocteau first spied Colette, her husband Willy, and her celebrated bulldog. New imports from America added another brand of excitement, including Negro jazz, which was rocking Parisian society, the boston, and the cake-walk.

But there were unpleasant events that marred the lad's joyous world: the wrenching death of Cocteau's father in 1899. The young Cocteau had been deeply attached to this gentle and soft-spoken man whose great love in life had been painting. Years later, Cocteau intimated— but this could be fabrication—that his father had committed suicide.

School was also a painful and "sinister" experience for the sensitive Cocteau. He loathed the institution to which he was sent: the "guillotinelike" awakenings in the morning, the dismal classrooms and teachers who inspired nothing but fear in him. For his sloppy notebooks and poor preparation he received ample rewards: *pensums* and other punishments. He was apparently the perfect example of what a schoolboy should *not* be like. His despairing mother hired private tutors, but to no avail. Cocteau's repressed hostilities were released every now and then during recreation periods in the schoolyard when he would fight with his school chums or throw snowballs. These episodes, full of fright, fantasy, anger, and joy were described with fidelity, though given symbolic overtones, in Cocteau's novel *Children of the Game (Les enfants terribles)* and in his film *The Blood of a Poet (Le Sang d'un poète).* There were other, perhaps more constructive activities that also relieved the youngster's tensions. When recuperating from the usual childhood diseases (scarlet fever, measles, and the like) he would build a small theater with lights, a ramp, and curtains. His German governess would sew the costumes, and he would create his own marvelous, magical world.

Cocteau's lack of aptitude for study did not indicate lack of intelligence or creativity. On the contrary, as he grew older, and the outer world about him assumed uglier proportions, his own inner flame glowed ever more brightly. He began writing poetry, for he felt compelled to express himself and this medium seemed ideal at the time. He wrote at a surprisingly fast pace. Indeed, his first volume of verse, *Aladdin's Lamp (La Lampe d'Aladin,* 1909) was published when he was sixteen; two volumes followed quickly, *The Frivolous Prince (Le prince frivole,* 1910) and *Sophocles' Dance (La Danse de Sophocles,* 1912).[2]

The poet's humor and affability attracted many friends, among them, François Mauriac, the future writer of novels such as *Génitrix, The Nest of Vipers (Le Noeud de vipères),* whose horrendous characters emerged full-grown from a troubled unconscious; Alain Fournier, the author of the highly poetic and elegantly structured novel *The Great Meaulnes (Le Grand Méaulnes)* that was to captivate a whole generation; and Claude Casimir-Périer. Indeed, Cocteau thrived on charming people, on being the center of attention. These characteristics, unconscious at first, were to become accentuated as time progressed.

Cocteau's friend René Rocher, the future director of the Théâtre Antoine and the Théâtre du Vieux-Colombier, introduced him to the celebrated actor Edouard de Max, star of the Comédie-Française, who was entranced by the young man's demeanor and talent. In fact, he was as addicted to young and "pretty" ephebes as he was to opium. Cocteau, in turn, was beguiled by de Max's kind and generous manner and fascinated by his apartment, which resembled a gypsy caravan, a combination of disorderliness and sumptuousness—a mysterious and tantalizing domain, certainly the kingdom of some powerful sultan or pasha.

It was de Max who organized and paid for public reading of Cocteau's poems at the Théâtre Femina (1906), to which a distinguished audience of well-known actors and actresses were invited. The most dreaded critics of the day praised Cocteau's literary endeavors lavishly; Catulle-Mendès, who rendered his verdict in the *Journal;* Laurent Tailhade, whose acidulous pen drove many a reader of the *Aurore* to desperation; Maurice Barrès, whose article was extremely favorable. Success was assured. Invitations poured in: from Jules Lemaître, whose *Impressions of the Theatre* remains, to this day, a clear, witty, and incisive commentary of theatrical events in his time; the Countess Anna de Noailles, author of voluptuous and melancholy verses that accounted to a great extent for her long list of admirers; Edmond Rostand, the creator of *Cyrano de Bergerac;* Lucien Daudet; the composer Raynaldo Hahn; and Marcel Proust. In 1906 Cocteau founded a literary magazine, *Schéhérazade,* with his friend François Bernouard and Maurice Rostand, the son of the famed dramatist, and a poet dramatist and novelist in his own right.

Cocteau had won a certain amount of acclaim. He also achieved his maturity. He slipped out from under his mother's hold and in 1912 moved into a wing of the Hotel Biron on the Rue Varenne. There he felt himself to be in good company, since the elegant central pavilion of this mansion was occupied by Auguste Rodin. At night, when he sat in his room writing poetry, nourishing dreams of fame and adulation, he frequently looked out, across the way, to another light burning brightly, that of Rodin's secretary, the young Rainer Maria Rilke.

A shocking occurrence, however, terminated Cocteau's dream of budding glory. Henri Ghéon, seconded by André Gide, wrote a stinging appraisal of his poems in the *Nouvelle Revue Française.* Praising his talent, they warned him in no uncertain terms of the treacherous nature of facile success. Characteristically, Cocteau immediately went to see Ghéon, thanked him for his constructive criticisms, and the confidence he had in his talent—but mostly, for having opened his eyes. Deep down, Cocteau must have known that his poems were not original, but rather a pastiche of every influence he had ever experienced, a hash of clichés. It was time for him to assess seriously his worth and his future, to look within and to discard the flitting charmer, the captivating dandy.

The young Cocteau realized that until now he had only played at being a literary figure. He was at the crossroads; a Narcissus ready to submerge into the pool's depths. But would it be only in hot pursuit of his own image? Or would he try to know himself *plain,* to search out and discover the whole of man?

The struggle was beginning. Cocteau was ready to wrestle with his fragmented personality, to fight to salvage what was best and mold it into a creative force.

He had always needed a catalyst to spur him on, an influence to excite him, a thought to provoke him and stimulate his own. Serge Diaghilev, founder of the Russian Ballet whom Cocteau met in 1912, became this external agent; he transformed the frivolous, extroverted, talented young man into the thoughtful, inventive, and eloquent poet he later became.

Cocteau was deeply impressed by Diaghilev, a tireless worker who constantly searched for new talents and techniques; attracting to his fold such composers as Claude Debussy, Igor Stravinsky, Maurice Ravel, and the members of "The Six," as they were later called (Georges Auric, Arthur Honegger, Darius Milhaud, Francis Poulenc, Germaine Taillefer, and Louis Durey). His sound judgment, thoroughness, and impeccable taste conquered Paris's elite. The elegance of Diaghilev's production of *Schéhérazade* featuring the extraordinary Nijinsky won immediate acclaim. Not so, however, with Stravinsky's *Rite of Spring* (1913), also produced by Diaghilev. It provoked a near riot as Paris gasped with horror at the "barbaric" cacophony emanating from the orchestra pit. Diaghilev, however, was not deterred.

Cocteau learned from the Diaghilev and Stravinsky setback that instant adulation by le tout Paris was not a reliable barometer of artistic worth. Toil, depth of feeling, and sincerity were what counted. Breaking former ties, Cocteau withdrew from society. He went to live in the house of his birth at Maisons-Lafitte; then he moved to Offranville, to the home of the future portrait painter Jacques Emile Blanche; the third and last step of his *ascesis* was spent at Leysen, Switzerland, with the Stravinskys. An original and fascinating collection of drawings, poems, and prose dialogues, dedicated to Stravinsky, was the outcome of this seclusion: *The Potomak* (*Le Potomak*).

At this juncture World War I erupted. Intensely patriotic, Cocteau volunteered to serve in the French army but was rejected on medical grounds. Notwithstanding, he served illegally as an ambulance driver on the Belgian front. Discovered by the authorities, Cocteau was returned to Paris posthaste. He later transformed this experience into a poetic, highly personal, and poignant novel, *The Impostor* (*Thomas l'Imposteur*, 1923).

To escape his feelings of depression and ineffectiveness, he sought thrills and excitement and so accepted with great alacrity the invitation of the stunt aviator Roland Garros to fly with him. Above the earth, free and riding high, Cocteau acquired a new perspective on life, a sense of possession and near-fulfillment, which he expressed in *The Cape of Good Hope* (*Le Cap de Bonne-Ésperance*), a volume of poetry much admired by Paul Claudel. Cocteau, in this work, created a new myth; he dealt with the plane as a living entity, as the means of new discovery and danger—a sort of mechanical Christopher Columbus.

The year 1916 was an important one for Cocteau. He gained entry into a new world peopled with the most exciting writers and artists of his generation. He met Amedeo Modigliani, whose slender figures were so reminiscent of Cretan paintings, a man who lived with the physical pain of hunger and the spiritual agony of total rejection by his contemporaries. He was introduced to Picasso. This meeting, Cocteau later wrote, was the "most" important encounter in his life.[3] Picasso was a man capable of everything, of turning anything he touched into a masterpiece: canvas, paper, clay, cardboard, paint, tin, iron. Like Orpheus, Cocteau affirmed, Picasso charmed objects; like Hercules, he was a "cyclone who twists iron." Picasso was a man possessed of clairvoyance.

Clairvoyance dominates his work. It would dry up a small spring. Now, it saves its strength and directs the flow. Its abundance does not occasion any romanticism. Inspiration does not overflow. Nothing remains to take or to leave. Harlequin lives in Port-Royal. Each work is drawn from intimate tragedy, resulting in calm intensity.[4]

Since 1904 Picasso had been living at the Bateau-Lavoir ("floating laundry"), a ramshackle building in Montmartre. It was there that he had begun painting what many critics consider to be the first cubist work "Les Demoiselles d'Avignon" (1907). By 1911–12, with such paintings as "Ma Jolie," Picasso was depicting forms that were no longer recognizable. A year later in 1913–14, Picasso and Braque began experimenting with textures instead of trying to reproduce them by means of various types of paint. They used actual pieces of newspaper, wallpaper, oilcloth, and fabrics of all types. This new technique was called *collage* and at first, the artists kept the motif element in the painting. Little by little, however, they worked out sculptural representations of these same objects, and by 1914 Picasso had built a three-dimensional still life with things he had picked up in his studio, in cafés, and in the street. Cocteau spent long hours with Picasso. Impressed by his spirit, his creativity, he learned that there need be no limits to the artists' means of expression, that one is constricted only by the boundaries of one's own imagination.

Guillaume Apollinaire, the ebullient playwright and poet, spokesman for the cubists, author of the riot-provoking play *Tirésias' Breasts* (*Les Mamelles de Tirésias*), also became Cocteau's close friend, as did the poets Max Jacob, Paul Reverdy, and André Salmon. With Blaise Cendrars, Cocteau founded Les Editions de la Sirène (1918). Intensely creative, the above-mentioned artists and writers stimulated Cocteau tremendously, arousing in him both fascinating and daring ideas.

Cocteau introduced Picasso to Diaghilev, and from this meeting was born the fabulous ballet *Parade* (1917). The argument for this ballet was composed by Cocteau, the music by Erik Satie, the sets and costumes by Picasso. The jarring colors and bizarre shapes of the sets and costumes, the atonal music, and the ambiguity of meaning in the argument were taken as insults by the audience. The shocked spectators felt they were witnessing a repudiation of everything they had learned to love since childhood. *Parade* created a veritable scandal. Had it not been for the presence of Guillaume Apollinaire, in military uniform and recuperating from a severe head wound, the authors of the ballet would have been physically attacked. As it was, they barely succeeded in escaping the wrath of the "Bacchae-like" spectators.

*Parade* was a flame-thrower, searing a path for an aggressive period in modern art. Cocteau now took his turn, and spoke out bluntly in a slim volume *The Rooster and the Harlequin* (*Le Coq et l'arlequin,* 1918). Pleading for an audacious and more simple music, he rejected the influences of such composers as Wagner, Debussy, and Stravinsky. He linked his aesthetics to that of "The Six." Needless to say, Cocteau's long essay created many enemies, the most important of whom was Igor Stravinsky, whose estrangement lasted until 1925. No matter. Cocteau felt free to express his ideas and he had something to say. Indeed, he was even more outspoken in a column he wrote in *Paris-Midi* entitled "Carte Blanche" (31 March–11 August 1919). According to Ned Rorem, "More than any other writer who ever lived, Cocteau worked *with* musicians; but for him, a great deal of worthwhile music would never have come into being."[5]

The year 1919 marked another new beginning for Cocteau. He was thirty years old and met the great love of his life, the fifteen-year-old Raymond Radiguet, future author of *The Devil in the Flesh* (*Le Diable au corps*). This young man whom Cocteau considered a genius was to play an important role in the poet's aesthetics. He changed the artistic course of the older man, influencing him to develop a classical, simple, and direct means of expression—never to float leisurely on the waves of popular artistic trends of the day but instead to work strongly and against the current, to look upon the seventeenth-century novel *The Princess of Clèves* (*La Princess de Clèves*) as a model of genuine literary art, to use meditation and solitude in a fruitful way. This unique friendship brought a new period of feverish creativity for Cocteau. He wrote a pantomime, *The Do-Nothing Bar* (*Le Boeuf sur le toit*, 1920), performed by the famed clowns, the Fratellini brothers, with masks and sets by Raoul Dufy and music by Darius Milhaud, a play, *The Wedding on the Eiffel Tower* (*Les Mariés de la Tour Eiffel*, 1921), in many ways a repudiation of modernism; a novel, *The Great Split* (*Le Grand Ecart*, 1923); poems, *Plain-Chant* (1922); and other works.

On 13 December 1923 Raymond Radiguet died of typhoid fever at the age of twenty-one. Now Cocteau was to experience deep pain for the first time. Life seemed unendurable. His emotional and physical state grew so desperate that Serge Diaghilev took him to Monte Carlo, hoping that an altered environment would help him. It was a failure. In fact, it was here that Cocteau found the only panacea available to him: opium. After prolonged taking of this drug, his friends and family convinced him to enter a sanatorium (Thermes urbain) on Rue de Chateaubriand in 1925. There he remained for sixty days and cured himself of the drug habit for the time being. It was at this period that the famed Thomist philosopher, Jacques Maritain, paid his first visit to Cocteau.

Jacques Maritain, convinced that faith was a cureall for pain, and seconded by Father Charles Henrion, succeeding in bringing the ailing poet back to the Catholic fold. But Cocteau's religiosity was of short duration; in the end, he rejected dogma. Two lengthly letters, the first by Cocteau, "Letter to Maritain," the second by Maritain, "Answer to Jean Cocteau," attest to the poet's spiritual search.

Maritain had a salutary influence on Cocteau. He helped him to regain a will to live, to clarify his aesthetic and philosophical ideas and the purposes of his future work. Cocteau was able to embark on a new phase, producing such works as "The Angel Heurtebise" ("L'Ange Heurtebise," 1925), the oratorio *Oedipus Rex* written in collaboration with Stravinsky (1925), *Orpheus* (*Orphée*, 1927), *Children of the Game* (*Les Enfants terribles*, 1929), and *Opium* (1930).

The Hotel Welcome at Villefranche-sur-Mer, a small town near Nice, offered Cocteau a sense of repose. There, in what he considered to be an idyllic spot, he relaxed into the tranquil atmosphere of southern France. From his hotel room, which looked right on to the Mediterranean, he watched the fishermen's activities by day and at night and walked along the busy little pier full of tourists and artists. The yellow-gold of the buildings, the greens of the palms and exotic plants lining the streets, the red rock shining against the glistening blue sky were conducive to Cocteau's well-being. It was at the Hotel Welcome that Cocteau met the artist Christian Bérard who would later create the décor for some of his plays; it was here too that he wrote his famed play *Orpheus,* composed much of the text for *Oedipus Rex,* and drew endless pictures of himself, his friends, and illustrations for his various books. Cocteau had always loved to draw, even in the early days when he filled his class notebooks, not with words, but with fanciful designs. The ease and grace of his lines, his ability to summon a personality in a few brash strokes, and his humor and incisiveness made him an artist of repute. In addition to being a gifted writer and artist, Cocteau was also to become a director (his adaptation of *Romeo and Juliet*), an actor (Mercutio), and an adapter of Greek tragedies (*Antigone*). The protean Cocteau was the first to modernize ancient tragedies, to adapt or paraphrase them for today's audiences.

Cocteau had matured. Aware that great art is the result of an exacting and profound search, that a fragmented and frivolous attitude is as destructive as a depressed one, Cocteau now seemed inexhaustible. In Paris, in his new apartment at 10 Rue Vignon, he wrote poems, plays (*The Infernal Machine* [*La Machine infernale,* 1932]), songs, ballets, art criticism (*Essay on Indirect Criticism* [*Essai de Critique indirecte,* 1932]), articles for *Figaro* (*Portraits-souvenir,* 1932), a regular column for *Ce Soir* (1937–38). Even this output did not fulfill Cocteau. He was going to try his hand at a new art—the film. *The Blood of a Poet* (1931), Cocteau's first motion picture, remains even today an outstanding artistic, exciting, and versatile work—a classic of its kind. When he took a trip around the world as the outcome of a bet with *Paris Soir,* he entitled the log he kept after Jules Verne's novel *Around the World in 80 Days.* Prizefighting also attracted Cocteau, and he became Alphonse Theo Brown's manager, encouraging him to win back his bantamweight title. Kindly toward others, Cocteau paved the way for Jean Marais's future theatrical and cinematographic career with *Oedipus Rex* and *The Knights of the Round Table* (*Les Chevaliers de la table ronde,* 1937).

Cocteau had earned international fame. His frenetic pace introduced both happy and unhappy results. His play *Intimate Relations* (*Les Parents terribles,* 1938) was banned by the Municipal Council on grounds of immorality. Despite such an interdiction, it was favored by le tout Paris. He took out the cudgel once again by writing plays, more poetic and poignant, more solid than the usual Boulevard productions: *The Holy Terrors (Les Monstres sacrés,* 1939), *The Typewriter (La Machine à écrire,* 1940), and a tragedy in verse, *Renaud and Armide* (1941).

During the German occupation of France, working in an unremitting manner was not really possible. Cocteau was now attacked from both French and German sources. His play *The Typewriter* was forbidden; the revival of *Intimate Relations* unleashed a series of jarring invectives on the part of journalists and politicians; he was finally beaten on the Avenue des Champs-Elysées by members of the fascist group Ligue des Volontaires Français for not saluting the flag.

Cocteau fought on all fronts, refusing to yield to any pressure groups either during the German Occupation or after the Liberation. He directed and wrote a series of movies: *The Eternal Return (L'Eternel retour,* 1942), based on the Tristan and Isolde legend; *Beauty and the Beast (La Belle et la bête,* 1945), an adaptation of an ancient fairy tale; *Orpheus* (1947), a film version of the play. He testified in favor of Jean Genet at the Court of Justice (1942). He designed an Aubusson tapestry featuring Judith and Holofernes (1948). He wrote the plays *The Eagle with Two Heads (L'Aigle a deux têtes,* 1946) and *Bacchus* (1951) and the collection of poems *Clear-Obscure* (1953). He wrote the essay collection *The Journal of One Unknown (Journal d'un inconnu,* 1952) and chronicles of his tours, *Maalesh* (1949), and travels, "Letters to Americans" (1949). He designed frescoes for the City Hall at Menton, the Chapel of Saint Pierre at Villefranche-sur-Mer, the Chapel of Notre Dame in London (1958), the church of Saint Blaise-des-Simples at Milly-la-Forêt (1959), where he had been living since 1947. His output of graphics was great and he left one hundred and fifty drawings to decorate a Chapel at Fréjus, Notre-Dame-de-Jerusalem, which his adopted son, Edouard Dermit, carried out after his death. Included in this list should be the recording Cocteau made; a mimodrama written in collaboration with Gian-Carlo Menotti and presented at Spoleto, Italy; and designs for plates, posters, fabrics, and the like.

The year was 1963 and Cocteau was seventy-four years old. His activity was still unremitting, but during moments of quiescence he was haunted by an old theme—a preoccupation with death. He wrote that as a youth he had feared it, but now he seemed to be invaded by a sensation of acceptance. It was almost as though nature were paving the way, beckoning the poet to follow her into the ultimate mystery. On 11 October, a Friday—only four hours after he had learned of his great friend Edith Piaf's passing—he told his housekeeper Juliette that he was not feeling well and that she would never again see him alive. Later that day, Cocteau took the giant leap down the path so many of his characters had followed—he stepped courageously and silently from one world to another.

## Chapter Two

# Scandal . . . Scandal . . .

## 1912–19

*For reality alone, even well disguised, has the power to move.*[1]

One evening in 1912, Diaghilev, Nijinsky, and Cocteau were on the Place de la Concorde, walking home at a leisurely pace after their dinner. Cocteau was quick to notice the Russian impresario's reserve. He asked him whether his attitude toward him had altered in any way. Adjusting his monocle, Diaghilev replied: "Astound me. . . ."[2] Cocteau was intrigued by the idea. He understood at once the exact meaning of the statement.

Clearly the Russian impresario had not been overly impressed by Cocteau's too-facile verses, *Aladdin's Lamp,* for example. Indeed, he trembled for his future. A poet must toil and search within, he insisted; superficial or vicarious experiences were not enough. Cocteau, previously warned about his glibness by Ghéon and Stravinsky, and now by Diaghilev, tried to take stock.

He was cognizant of his talent, of his ability to write charming, imagistic, and melodious verse. But he wondered how all these natural talents would develop? Would they be stunted? Cut off by sheer lack of perseverance, or worse, by a shallow fragmented pesonality that had caused him to splash his talents around indiscriminately? Something was missing in his work, as it was in his life, he concluded. Only through a concentrated inner search could he perhaps understand and unify the multiple aspects of his own personality and thereby find direction.

Cocteau had an idea now for a work, but he did not really know how to go about bringing it to fruition. He wanted to write a novel of some sort; unorthodox, strictly personal, one that would come from his inner depths and be plainly *his.* A self-imposed exile was in order; Cocteau cut himself off from a society that had been so lavish with its laudatory attention: Edmond Rostand, Anna de Noailles, Lucien Daudet, Maurice Barrès. Alone, Cocteau found the inner peace necessary to compose his strange and revelatory work labeled by some a novel, an *ars poetica* by others: *The Potomak* (1913).

## *The Potomak*

. . . . here I am, something totally machine-like, totally antenna-like, totally Morse-like. A Stradivarius of the barometer. A tuning-fork. A Central Bureau for phenomena.[3]

The slim volume *The Potomak* includes poems, prose, letters, dialogues, drawings, and confessions. It not only totally ignores all the literary and artistic trends of the day, but reacts courageously against them, particularly to the maudlin and sentimental novel. Cocteau substitutes for the "well-made" novel with its rationally conceived plots and flesh-and-blood characters, a plotless and irrational work in which the reader has great difficulty finding his bearings. The plot, therefore, will merely be touched upon here.

*The Potomak's* main figure, the narrator, inhabits a chaotic world, along with a whole series of allegorical beings who are forever emerging from nowhere only to exit into a void. Speaking in frequently cryptic terms, the narrator recalls his past in a totally illogical manner and with no apparent relationship to his present acts. Time seems to be congealed and space has become porous.

The characters in *The Potomak*—Persicaire, Argemone (his name was taken from the label on a medicine bottle Cocteau saw in a pharmacy in Normandy), Bourdaine, the Eugenes, the Mortimers and others—act and react in a series of seemingly disconnected sequences. But as the narrator explains, since these formless substances came to him from his inner world, unexpectedly and without any "pedigree," he feels compelled to describe them as they flow forth from his depths.

Because *The Potomak* is written largely in a stream-of-consciousness style, the feeling of apprehension and anguish within its pages is readily discernible. A true distortion of reality à la grotesque *Alice in Wonderland* is also implicit in this work, and as a result, cruelty, satire, fantasy, and ugliness seem to radiate forth.

One problem that seems to have haunted Cocteau at this period and explains, partially at least, the reason for the narrator's torment throughout the pages of *The Potomak* is the question of originality. Indeed, the narrator's search for originality becomes one of this work's basic themes. In fact, Bourdaine, who frequently acts as the narrator's mentor, suggests he concentrate his sensibilities in *one* single area. In this manner, he claims, the narrator will be able to reach the core of his problem, rather than remain on the periphery. Anxieties are also manifested in the various monstrous forms and beings with whom the narrator comes into contact. Most of these elemental entities suffer from sexual anomalies in their most blatant forms. The human body appears in fantastic and terrifying proportions. To make matters even more disorienting, "phosphorescent" fish of all shapes and sizes, strange sea shells, the face of a woman with one large eye, a round ear, a "Eugene," as Cocteau called them, made of an unformed mass, a yellow book, and an ink bottle—emerge from dimly lit airless caverns of the narrator's unconscious. All these hallucinatory objects relate, symbolically speaking, in one way or another, to Cocteau's own basic sense of peril, the danger he felt awaited him if he did not succeed in giving birth to something unique and pleasing to his audiences.

*The Potomak* is also in a sense, an *ars poetica* in which Cocteau comes to certain conclusions as to the poet's situation in general. The poet, Cocteau feels, must have faith in his mission.

> Have faith in your role
> And if you create
> Do not become a spectator,
> Carry your secret
> And sacred trust any place. . . .[4]

The poet is also a hierophant, a translator of secret and universal mysteries. Influenced by Baudelaire and Rimbaud, Cocteau believed that the writer must dredge his own murky depths to find truth as well as his own identity. He must then reveal his findings in cryptic lines that will make up his future work of art. "I exploit the void . . ." Cocteau declared.[5] The poet then acts as an intermediary between the world of the living and the dead, a *seer* in the Rimbaudian sense, a visionary, a magician who can render the concrete invisible and the amorphous palpable.

*The Potomak* is also, in a sense, an *ars poetica* in which its covers are sixty-four drawings executed by Cocteau. He entitles this section of the book the "Album of the Eugenes." Although each drawing is different, the figures portrayed have certain common characteristics. They are fat, frequently one-eyed, with Negroid features, and are triangular in shape. The abstract nature of the subjects gives them a sculptural quality. It could be said that Cocteau's imagination had been stirred by Alfred Jarry's depiction of King Ubu, his childlike and naïve expressions, his humor and satire. A sense of the grotesque and a flair for caricature in Cocteau's drawings indicate traces of Daumier and of Toulouse-Lautrec. A certain aggressive and violent quality in the Fauve paintings of Matisse and Dufy are also discernible in Cocteau's sketches. There is no doubt that Cocteau was a good draftsman, that he succeeded in capturing certain facets of the human personality, most frequently their distorted and sordid sides.

Like André Gide's *The Fruits of the Earth,* Cocteau's *The Potomak* is a "profession of faith" in life, in work; it is also a quest for adventure. It expresses a desire to communicate, to reveal to the reader the author's deepest turmoils.

Modesty impels us to treat our profoundest worries lightly. This same modesty prevents people from listening to us, from taking us seriously. I masked the drama which is taking place in *The Potomak* under a thousand different faces. So we sing, to give us courage in the dark.[6]

Rebelling against the picturesque and the romantic novels popular in some literary and artistic circles, Cocteau chose to express his feelings and torments in a detached and objective manner, as though they had come from another part of himself. The stream-of-consciousness style that he adopted in *The Potomak,* first used by William James in his *Principles of Psychology* (1890), permitted Coteau to describe, by means of a series of symbols, motifs, and associations, a world that is considered incoherent on the surface but possesses its own inner logic. The "interior monologue," first used by Edouard Dujardin in *We'll to the Woods No More,* was adopted by Cocteau to a certain extent and permitted him slightly more rational control over the unconscious content that poured from him. These devices, coupled with the changes he effected in puctuation, syntax, and typography, reflect a whole new concept of aesthetics that had come into being at the turn of the century.

Cocteau, therefore, had broken with the much adulated writers of his day. He did not imitate the antinaturalist novelist Maurice Barrès, for example, the man who had set the style for the *"culte du moi,"* the defender of public order, whose novel *The Uprooted (Les Déracinés,* 1897) had encouraged countless young Frenchmen to rally around his conservative bannner. Nor did he try to emulate Paul Bourget's thesis novel *The Disciple* (1898), which championed tradition and sought to mock and destroy anything that smacked of novelty. Anatole France, the humanitarian, the militant Socialist, who deprecated "the crudities of the naturalists" as well as the "obscurities of the symbolists," did not serve as Cocteau's model either in such a work as *At the Sign of Queen Pédauque* (1893). Nor did Romain Rolland, author of *Jean Christophe* (1904–12), the idealist who sought to rekindle a heroic faith in his nation, have any effect upon Cocteau's writings. But the works of both Gide and Proust, pivotal influences to a whole generation, did catch Cocteau's fancy.

Gide, most frequently the source and subject of his own work, tried to disinter his own deepest conflicts and suppressed desires. He was determined to free himself of all the constraints imposed upon him in his rigorous and unhappy childhood. Cocteau would try to do likewise, but only up to a certain point. When Gide advised young people to leave their homes and families, to live fervently, and pass from one exciting experience to the next, Cocteau suggested some other answer. "Remain. Rush as speedily as possible right into your own depths."[7] There was, in fact, even at this early date, a clash of temperaments that would broaden in time, that accounted for these opposing points of view. Yet Gide had taught Cocteau an important lesson: to banish all traces of self-pity from his writing and to face situations directly and never in an involved style.

Proust's influence upon Cocteau was also manifest. A man who had transmuted his emotional and philosophical life-experience into his novel *Swann's Way* (1913), Proust had created something absolutely unique in the annals of literature. Cocteau admired him and they became good friends. They saw each other at the home of Mme Alphonse Daudet, at dinner parties and in the cork-lined room to which Proust retreated when his asthma had become too severe. There is no doubt that Proust's self-analytical literary technique encouraged and stimulated Cocteau into a similar adventure.

Strangely enough, the man to whom Cocteau felt he owed the greatest debt at this period was not a writer, but a composer, Igor Stravinsky, to whom he had dedicated *The Potomak:* "When I wrote *The Potomak* I was incapable of seeing into my malaises; Stravinsky helped me come out of it as a box of cheddite releases ore."[8] Stravinsky's music had a profound effect upon Cocteau's writings. Certain sections of *The*

*Potomak* that give the impression of opulence, theatricality, and a sense of the mythological had been inspired by Stravinsky's atonal and polytonal music. In fact, Cocteau confessed that parts of *The Potomak,* including the "Album of the Eugenes," had been written while actually listening to his master's music.

Despite the many trends and influences visible in *The Potomak,* it is a work that demonstrates Cocteau's interpretive and creative power at the threshold of his career. This dynamic and hallucinatory novel narrates a personal inner drama: Cocteau's flight from the society that had adulated him, and his descent into the mobile and mysterious world of his unconscious. To a great extent his former peripheral existence was over. He had taken seriously the story of the phoenix, related to him by Stravinsky, the mythical Arabian bird that burns itself alive and then is reborn with new life. Cocteau realized now that the birth of the *real* poet is difficult and painful. It must be considered with lucidity, accomplished in "secret," understood in depth. "There one sinks into one's self," wrote Cocteau, "toward the diamond, toward the fire-damp."[9]

## *The Discourse of the Great Sleep*

I have a piece of great and sad news to tell you: I am dead.[10]

Cocteau's literary endeavors were to be interrupted by World War I. After he had been plucked away from the Belgian front where he had been driving an ambulance, he was returned to Paris. There he learned that the Marine company to which had been very close (at Neiuport, Belgium) had been wiped out just the day after he had been forced to leave his post. This experience had stirred him deeply and had provoked him to write *The Discourse of the Great Sleep* (*Discours du Grand Sommeil,* 1920).

*The Discourse of the Great Sleep* is the title given by Cocteau to a collection of eleven poems written between 1916 and 1918. These verses, which deal mostly with Cocteau's horrendous war experiences, take the reader into the trenches where the poet acquaints him with the workings of torture and death. *The Discourse of the Great Sleep* is the work of a young man angry at the endless suffering inherent in the human condition. But Cocteau's poems are not only antiwar polemics, they are also directed against accusations certain people had leveled at him at the time. Because of Cocteau's flippant, witty, and humorous manner—a true personality trait—they felt he harbored a callous attitude toward the war. The suffering of the soldiers, the spirit of sacrifice so many had demonstrated during France's traumatic hours, had not affected him, they claimed. Few realized that the off-handedness visible in Cocteau's demeanor was and would always be a mask, imposed upon himself during moments of extreme stress. This defense mechanism acted as a device for protecting his soft inner world from becoming visible and, thereby incurring even more pain. Should the outside world ever become cognizant of his extreme vulnerability, he could certainly be the butt of ridicule. Such an eventuality would be too searing, and Cocteau would prevent it at all costs.

The soldiers' world is painted in *The Discourse of the Great Sleep* in strong classical tones. The forbidding life in the trenches, the cold and wetness, the ice caking around the legs, the terrible fright when shells explode, and "The child of the North dies of fright"[11] are all incised in detail. The monotony and exhaustion during the endless marches, the doctors' harried efforts to alleviate pain, the silence, the screams of the agony of death are depicted in vibrant images. In the purely descriptive passages that make up certain sections of this work, Cocteau reveals his deep sense of sorrow, the trauma he was undergoing during the long days of perpetual anguish.

The theme of the Angel, so important in all of Cocteau's later undertakings, first emerges in these dazzling war poems. It is not the biblical Angel, Cocteau is quick to point out, to whom he refers in these verses:

> but the inner formless
> angel, which slumbers
> and, sometimes, softly
> stretches from top to bottom:
> He awakens![12]

The Angel is vaguely drawn, however, and represents many things to the poet: the unconscious, the Muse, poetry per se, a messenger from another world. The Angel speaks to the young man in varying tones: imperiously, cajolingly, tenderly, lovingly, trying to relieve him of his doubts and pain. He cannot assuage his wounds by eradicating the external holocaust, but he can make the anguish bearable, as had Musset's Muse, by listening to the poet, by prodding and encouraging him to express his pain.

The most arresting section of this work, made up of several pages in prose entitled "Visit," deals with Cocteau's growing preoccupation with death. He had seen so much of it during his period as an ambulance driver that now he compels himself to confront the force that has always terrorized him. At first, he personifies death, then he tries to analyze the meaning of that power which engulfs all of life; in jest, the poet even announces the news of his own demise. From the land of the dead, however, things appear unlike anything he had ever known before: time, speed, sound are conceived as altogether different entities. No longer limited by the intellectual concepts of the living, Cocteau is free to roam in his vast domain—and now with total vision.

We, we are not seen, we are not heard, we can be crossed without causing hurt. Our speed is so great that we are situated at a point in silence and monotony. I can come to you because I have not yet reached my full speed and fever has caused your speed to become immobile, something rarely experienced among the living.[13]

For Cocteau, poetry, like death, is part of an immeasurable spatial domain, incomprehensible to those who cannot immerse themselves in it both physically and spiritually, whose vision has been cut and altered by an "over-life."

## *The Cape of Good Hope* and *Vocabulary*

> I am elaborating
> in the prairies of inner
> silence[14]

It was in 1915, after Cocteau's unsuccessful war experience, that he met the aviator Roland Garros.[15] A friendship between the two men ensued, and the aviator took Cocteau with him from Villacoublay on his daily stunt flights. This exciting and totally new venture inspired Cocteau to write a whole volume of verse, *The Cape of Good Hope* (*Le Cap de Bonne-Ésperance*), featuring the airplane as the main image and the feelings, sensations, and thoughts it aroused in him. This work, which includes ten poems dedicated to Roland Garros, was published in 1919 by Sirène publications, a firm founded by Blaise Cendrars and Jean Cocteau.[16]

The airplane, as Cocteau conceives of it in *The Cape of Good Hope*, is a symbol for the modern age, an entity free from worldly ties, shorn of matter, delivered from the earth's grasping tentacles. It also represents man in a state of solitude, the individual versus the collective. The image of the plane, therefore, permits the poet to escape from a world of material restrictions as represented by the earth; to seek solitude in an etheral atmosphere in order to know his soul, but it also puts him face to face with one of the great hazards of unlimited freedom and of extreme solitude: to reject matter totally is to die. But the image of the returning plane, however, of its eventual landing on earth, also featured in *The Cape of Good Hope,* implies reintegration, a return to the world of the living.

The most unusual aspect of the poems appearing in *The Cape of Good Hope* is not only in the aerial adventure that they relate, but the sensual impressions they create upon the reader. Indeed, he actually feels himself in the plane with the author. The poems seem to lunge forth from the written page and at a dazzlingly swift pace, revealing a series of panoramic visions during their flight, then strike hard with cutting images and abrasive sounds as they soar through the atmosphere before falling back into oblivion.

In "Preamble" the description of the countryside is recounted in terse, elliptical, and graceful phrases: the chattering chickens, the barking dogs, the screech of the swallows filling the atmosphere with nostalgia, the evening descending upon a farm, clothing it in crisp colors, the plane looming forth as if from an ocean, with speed and fury:

> There is not a minute to lose
>
> The roosters
> this hubbub from limbo
> this
> barking of fleeing phantoms
> around the church       the angelus
> the hamlet
> is giving birth      it
>            is pale it is frightened.

And a feeling of exhilaration fills the poet's lungs as he surges through the air in his machine.

The plane, now personfied, becomes the harbinger of dreams, of freedom. It looks down upon the ground, the greenery, plants, flowers, and trees bursting into bloom, germinating willy nilly—all prisoners of matter. Abstract and concrete notions fly by in chromatic tones: poetry, art, snow, luxury, countrysides at all seasons, the color white. The shock of descent forces the poet to take hold of his senses; he feels his solitude as did Columbus "before a mirrored closet" and the coldness, the isolation, the agony of the void startles the traveler. He shudders. Exploring this semiconscious state, looking back into the depths of his being, a reflection of the world that shimmers before him, he listens to the sorrowful incantations emanating from within him, and the poet now begins his struggle against deafness and blindness, for he has decided now to wrestle with the poem he seeks to create.

In his glistening plane he spirals upward anew, listening intently. His ear has now become a highly sensitive instrument, recording the beat and hum of universal cosmic forces. The poet sees himself in his plane as a column of smoke rising up into infinity "As an ear listens to a seashell" and his eye peers from within "against a crystal paper weight." He has learned to penetrate matter, to understand the unknown. Strength has filled his muscles, and the poem, like the androgyne, has grown from itself.

"Attempt to escape" ("Tentative d'évasion") also begins from the heights and depicts another view of the land: the crisp countryside as the farmer turns over his soil to make it ready for the spring planting. A prisoner of the earth, restrained by an unsevered umbilical cord, the farmer and man in general, toils and labors trying to fructify what is at hand:

> Heavy heavy
> despotic tufa
>
> With a single kiss the mother crushes
> the prodigal son

The poet, however, is unlike the farmer. He is a traveler, wandering as does the plane over the waters and through the skies. He looks upon the plane as an "adorable giant," with its grinding propellers cutting into space; its humming engine, breathing its inhuman breath, with an urge to bite and to sear, confronts "The music of the stars." To make his image more effective, Cocteau includes a series of onomatopoetic vowels to give the reader the illusion of actually experiencing the sensations of being rocked and surrounded by blaring heavens and glistening shades and forms:

| eo | ie | iu | ie |
|----|----|----|-------|
| e  | e  | iu | io ie |

Cocteau's volume of poetry entitled *Vocabulary* (*Vocabulaire*, 1922) written between the years 1918 and 1919, is thought-provoking because of the philosophical insights he reveals in it. These thoughts are important at this juncture not only because they reveal Cocteau's preoccupations, but because they will help the reader understand the more subtle aspect of some of his later works such as *Orpheus*.

The belief in cosmic flux, taught by the priests in the ancient Egyptian mystery schools, by the Platonists, the Gnostics, and the mystics in general, was part and parcel of Cocteau's conceptions. Cocteau envisaged the cosmos as an entity in a state of perpetual transformation, moving from primordial unity to differentiation and back again to the original state. Death in this universal cycle was considered to be a transitory period, an initiation into another phase of existence. The poems in *Vocabulaire* are a literary reflection of these beliefs. Images for Cocteau, therefore, such as the statue, salt, pearl, and snow can be looked upon as momentary, material manifestations of other elements in the cosmos imperceptible and incomprehensible to the human mind and eye, emblems or symbols accruing to man from other stages of life. A statue, for example, is transformed by Cocteau in one poem into salt and the salt into flesh; a pearl and snow undergo similar metamorphoses as do a flower, a clown, and a fan. According to Cocteau, the poem itself experiences similar vicissitudes. It emerges from limbo, lives as long as there is someone to read it, then vanishes into another realm where it survives in a form foreign to human comprehension.

The process of change, in initiation from one state to another, or from life to death, can be terribly painful. In "Death of a Swan" ("Mort d'un cygne"), for example, inspired most certainly by Mallarmé's poem treating a similar image, Cocteau describes people in a boat holding on to something they believe to be a tangible entity, a statue of a swan made of salt. But it is in fact dead matter and slips away silently into another shape, just as youth blends into age, almost imperceptibly. While one metamorphosis takes place on earth, the poet looks up, toward the clouds, which in turn, reflecting various moods of the viewer, assume many shapes: a clown, a murderer, a horse.

In a different vein, there appears in this volume a series of poems entitled "Tombs" ("Tombeaux") in which Sappho, Socrates, and Narcissus express in one way or another the joys of homosexual love. One of the poems, "Birds Covered by Snow" ("Oiseaux sont en neige"), could be considered a veritable ode to homosexuality:

> Birds covered by snow and they change their sex.
> A bathrobe deceived our parents. . . .
> Inhuman, is it a crime after all? to meet again,
> Treasure of the cold wave where your hand bathes . . .

In "Right Side and Wrong Side" ("L'Endroit et l'envers") Cocteau blends the two main themes of this work: death (transformation) and homosexuality. This poem depicts the thirty-year-old poet who now sees himself as being midway in his journey through life. He looks back upon his youth, at all the memories fading away at a too-rapid pace and the mystery of what is to come; the land he will eventually reach inspires fright. The poet, however, who is susceptible and sensitive to the ephemeral and captivating aspects of worldly existence, is relieved from life's arduous labors at times through love and beauty.

Though *The Discourse of the Great Sleep, The Cape of Good Hope,* and *Vocabulary* vary considerably from Cocteau's earlier volumes of poetry (*Aladdin's Lamp, The Frivolous Prince, Sophocles' Dance*) and reveal a new technical mastery over this art form, a reflection of certain poetic trends of the day is indeed present. And this must be reviewed at this time.

The rigidity in prosody set down by the Parnassian poets had been rejected by a group of young writers, among whom were Guillaume Apollinaire, Max Jacob, and Blaise Cendrars. Influenced by Baudelaire, Rimbaud, Lautréamont, and Jarry, these new writers, using a different poetic technique, sought to expand their vision and to discover unchartered territories within the human soul. Apollinaire declared that just as painting could make use of any subject or object, so poetry should move out of pastoral sentimentality and into the centers of modern life with all of its machines and noises, its fire and energy.

Apollinaire, young and vital, was Cocteau's good friend. From him he absorbed the insights he used in *The Cape of Good Hope* and *Vocabulary* as well as his later poetic works. Cocteau, for example, discarded what he considered to be a constricting rational approach to verse in favor of images flowing directly from his unconscious. In this manner, he altered his visual conceptions of the world and so was able to

consider anything a subject worthy of poetry—even a plane. Furthermore, just as Apollinaire had combined free and classical verse forms (in
*Alcools*) and had used (in *Calligrammes*) actual words to draw lines,
injecting life, thereby, into typography itself, so Cocteau adopted this
same technique to suit his own verses.

Cubism, futurism, and dadaism were also forces that both activated
and changed the poetic aesthetics of the day—and Cocteau's aesthetics
as well. Cubism, with its geometricization of the universe, its concen-
tration on form, influenced Cocteau in his poetic endeavors in the
following manner: in the physical layout of his verses, which created
optical illusions for the reader; by the use of ellipses; by the breaking
down of conventional syntactical formations. In "The Parable of the
Prodigal Child" ("Parabole de l'enfant prodigue") appearing in *The Cape
of Good Hope,* one has the impression that Cocteau is splashing form on
canvas, particularly when describing such entities as trees, rocks, sea,
foam, sailboats, dunes, algae, furs, and the Mediterranean, that "funda-
mental mirror of the myth. . . ." It must be recalled too, that the
aesthetics of cubism had been analyzed by Apollinaire in *The Cubist
Painters* (written between 1911 and 1912; published in 1913) and
introduced by him into his own poetry, *Alcools,* published in that same
year. Max Jacob, a friend of Apollinaire, Picasso, and Cocteau as well,
displayed his "cubistic" verbal prowess in *Dice-Box* (1917), a work filled
with strange and provocative verbal images, word associations that
seem to tumble forth at a rapid pace from his tormented mind, assuming frequently abstract and sculptural forms. Blaise Cendrars, a bold
innovator in poetics, altered traditional rhythmic and syntactical struc-
tures by omitting punctuation and juxtaposing jarring verbal sounds.

The Futurist school of painters founded by Umberto Boccioni in
Turin (1910) likewise gave new direction to many French poets including Cocteau. Considering the universe as an entity made up of mobile
forms, the Futurists sought to express their notions of energy, time,
and space in both abstract and concrete terms. They felt that the
machine in many cases could best express the concept of "universal
dynamism" in which they believed. Cocteau was perhaps prompted by
the futurists to mechanical words in certain poems included in *The Cape
of Good Hope* among others: oil, piston, screw, any noun that strength-
ened or clarified the sensation or the image he sought to communicate.

The dadaists also played an important role in formulating the new
aesthetics. The dadaist movement, founded by Tristan Tzara in 1916,
sought to abolish laws, morality, and religion as well as systems, theo-

ries, and logic. Though dadaism was negative in essence, it did have a positive side. It believed inspiration, uncontrolled by the rational mind, to be the source of art. Such a notion appealed greatly to the rebellious Cocteau. He transformed this theory into a poetic technique that he used most effectively in his verse in expressing his contrasting moods, the calm and peaceful moments as opposed to the violent and corrosive periods. Cocteau juxtaposed his free-flowing emotions in his nature descriptions, thereby giving his poems drama and vigor.

Though one still finds traces of punning, of enigmatic statements in Cocteau's poetry, the sheer musicality of his language turns his writings into what could be called tone poems. The quality of elegance, the spontaneity of style, and the freshness implicit in *The Discourse of the Great Sleep, The Cape of Good Hope,* and *Vocabulary* all bode well for his future works. Embellishments are few, words are lean and devoid of accoutrements—they seem to glisten as does a nude moist body in the sun.

## Parade

I was never to know anything but scandals, a reputation for scandals, the luck and bad luck that come with scandals. [17]

Cocteau, as we have seen, was equally at home in the world of the painter, the writer, and the musician. When on furlough, back in 1915, he heard Erik Satie play his four-hand composition "Morceaux en forme de poire" with Ricardo Vines, he had been so impressed by this man's extreme sensitivity that he decided he must collaborate with him on some work. He felt a special bond for Satie because he had rebelled against the ideals of romanticism and had created a new kind of music that attracted the attention of "The Six." Before leaving for the front, Cocteau left a whole series of notes with Satie in which were included certain themes for what was to become the future ballet *Parade.*

It was not surprising that Cocteau should have been attracted to the ballet as an art form. Ever since he had met Diaghilev he had been enthralled by the music, dancing, and decor of the Ballet Russe. Cocteau had written his first ballet for Diaghilev, *The Blue God,* in 1912, with music by Raynaldo Hahn. This ballet was based on a Hindu fairy tale. Fokine's decor was influenced by sacred Hindu scripture; the choreography was reminiscent of the Siamese dancers he had seen in Russia years before. Though the critics had been impressed by the brash blue lights splashed on the stage, highlighting the extraordinary beauty of Nijinsky's gestures, his steps and pirouettes, Cocteau's ballet could not be called successful. He vowed he would write another one—some day.

The idea for *Parade* was not new. In fact, in the autumn of 1913, Cocteau had mentioned to Stravinsky a theme for a ballet to be entitled *David.* It was to take place at a fair and include an acrobat tumbling outside a booth and a clown, trying to lure the crowd inside to see the full show. Nothing came of Cocteau's idea at the time.[18]

Three years later, Cocteau introduced Picasso to Diaghilev and induced him to commission a ballet to be called *Parade,* with Picasso doing the costumes and decor; Erik Satie, the score; and Jean Cocteau, the argument and choreography. Picasso's acceptance of the commission created the first of the many "scandals" that were to mark the very eventful career of *Parade.*

Cocteau labeled *Parade* a "ballet-réaliste," meaning something "more real than the real" (*"plus vrai que le vrai"*).[19] The argument, as written by Cocteau, is uncomplicated and contrasted in this respect with the sumptuousness and intricacies of other works performed by the Russian Ballet. The action, a play within a play, takes place in Paris. It is Sunday. A side show is being performed in front of a play-crowd unwilling at all costs, to enter the play-theater, despite the fact that the evolving side show eventually becomes a real play enacted for a real audience.

Featured are a Chinese juggler and prestidigitator, danced by Massine, who nods and bows, breathes fire, makes an egg disappear; a Little American Girl, dressed in a sailor coat, white skirt, white knee stockings, and black shoes, who enters to the sound of the jazz tune, "The Steamship Rag," swims a river, drives a car, and flaunts a revolver; and acrobats, who perform their music-hall numbers. Three managers with immense cardboard heads, make their entrance, after which they begin stamping and stomping madly about, to the accompaniment of Satie's music, which was "neither major nor minor, neither tonal nor atonal." They give vent to their frustration in a frenzy of action and gesticulations, trying their best to convince the bystanders, to enter their theater since "The real show is on the inside." No one buys a ticket. No one goes in. Their efforts are in vain because the spectators are convinced that the "parade"—which consists of the managers' antics and the music-hall numbers—is the actual performance. The managers are so exhausted after their futile efforts that they fall down into a heap. The three performers emerge from an empty theater, see what has been going on, and try once again to attract the spectators inside the theater where the *real* performance is taking place.

Understood symbolically, *Parade* reveals the insensitivity of audiences and their unwillingness to open their minds to new artistic ventures, preferring the facile, the worn and dated conventional way to the dangers associated with the new and revolutionary path. It also suggests Cocteau's intense preoccupation with his inner being. The managers' antics, which could be interpreted as Cocteau's written work and his social life, try fervently to entice outsiders to look within, to communicate with him on a profounder level. Instead, however, people take the outer manifestation of his inner world at face value. They refuse to try harder, to listen, and to follow him to the dark and secret aspects of his existence. Since all the surface machinations are to no avail, the inner being remains alone.

Rehearsals for *Parade* took place in Leonide Massine's atelier and in the Cave Taglione. Here, too, Picasso put the finishing touches on his sets and costumes. The former included buildings, trees, and a barracks. A horsewoman, harlequins, guitarists, and a giant Pegasus were painted on the curtain in brilliant hues. The Chinaman wore a gaily colored costume in keeping with the various activities he had to pursue on stage, in which he took an egg from his braid, ate and digested it, picked it up from the tip of his sandal; spit fire, burned himself, and stamped out the sparks. The Little Girl's costume was grotesque, and her actions and gesticulations were reminiscent of Charlie Chaplin. She rode a bicycle on stage, chased a thief with a revolver, danced a ragtime, fell asleep, snapped a picture, and the like. The acrobats, painted blue, looked foolish yet agile; they wore melancholia (always present around circuses on Sunday nights) in their features. They led Marcel Proust to compare them, later, to the Dioscures.[20] Picasso's horse, which Mme de Noailles described in an article as a "laughing tree"[21] and Proust alluded to as "a great swan with mad gestures,"[22] was fantastic and humorous. As for the managers, they were more traditional, like "men-decor"—ferocious, vulgar, noisy, funny.[23]

Cocteau wanted audiences to laugh and to enjoy his work. In an article written for *l'Excelsior* and printed the day of *Parade*'s premiere, he wrote: "Our wish is that the public may consider *Parade* as a work that conceals poetry beneath the coarse outer skin of *guignol* . . . Laughter is natural to Frenchmen . . . Laughter is too Latin a weapon to be neglected."

Before Picasso created his sets for *Parade,* decor enjoyed no role in a

play, serving merely as background. Picasso's sets changed this proce-
dure. They were alive, vibrant, and set both pace and spirit to the
ballet.

Music also played an important part in *Parade*. Cocteau had originally wished to include a series of concrete sounds that would have
emanated from the orchestra pit: sirens, typewriters clicking, noise of
express trains, planes, and so on. Because of technical difficulties,
however, these additions were abandoned. The music Satie composed
for *Parade* was, in Cocteau's words, a masterpiece. It included a fugue,
three dances with numerous motifs, each distinct from the other. Unity
of tone, however, pervaded the entire work, linking all the themes and
emotions, arousing "unknown nostalgias. . . ."[24]

In Apollinaire's introduction in the program, he declared that Picasso and Massine had brought about "the alliance of painting and
dance, of music and the plastic arts, which is the sign of a more
complete art. From this new alliance has resulted something beyond
realism . . . surrealism." From Diaghilev, Cocteau had learned that for
mixed media to play an important role in the total work of art, it had to
be made of autonomous components.

*Parade,* an unconventional work, created one scandal after another.
The first concerned Picasso and the theatrical decor he had made for
this work. It must be recalled that the artists of Montparnasse and
Montmartre, removed from the theatrical world, considered the design-
ing of theatrical productions unworthy of their talents—a "crime" in
fact.[25] Indeed, a vritual dictatorship of what could and could not be
done in painting had been established by the cubists. It was, in Cocteau's words, the "austere period of Cubism." These artists had created
their own dogma—a virtual religion—and lived by it. For example,
they were permitted to paint only a Spanish guitar and those objects
that could be found on a table. Another rule: they held that no artist
could travel outside of Paris or beyond La Place des Abbesses to the
Boulevard Raspail in Paris.

When Diaghilev took his Ballet Russe to Rome in 1916, he and his
collaborator, Leonide Massine, asked Cocteau, Picasso, and Satie to
follow for the opening in *Parade*. Satie remained in Paris. Cocteau and
Picasso, however, went to Rome, leaving the other cubists in a state of
consternation. Such a move was not intended as a show of disrespect or
of a lessening of affection for the cubists; it merely set forth a belief that
the theater was one more way of expressing man's creative spirit. Picasso's acceptance of Diaghilev's offer paved the way, however, for other

artists (among them, Matisse, Braque, Dufy, Chagall) to contribute
their talents in years to come to the ballet, the opera, and the theater.
The second scandal came on opening night at the Théâtre du
Chatelet in Paris, 18 May 1917. The performance on stage lasted for
twenty minutes. After the finale, the "show" moved into the theater
itself. The audience jeered and hooted, accusing the artists of being
"Boches" ("Krauts"). Some merely screamed out their rage; others resorted to their fists. As Cocteau was crossing the hall with Apollinaire
to join Picasso and Satie who were waiting for them in a box, a fat lady
spotted Cocteau. She took out her hat pin, screeched, "There's one of
them," and lunged at Cocteau brandishing her weapon. It took
Apollinaire and the fat woman's husband to hold down this "bacchante"
and prevent her from puncturing his eyes.

Though Cocteau, Picasso, and Satie had been saved from bodily
harm, they were verbally flayed alive by the critics. In fact, on opening
night, Cocteau overheard a gentleman say: "If I had known it was going
to be so stupid, I would have brought my children."[26] André Gide
noted in his *Journal:*

. . . went to see Parade—one doesn't know what to admire most; its preten-
sion or its poverty. Cocteau is walking in the wings where I went to see him;
aging, contracted, pained. He knows very well that Picasso created the sets
and the costumes; Satie composed the music, but he wonders if Picasso and
Satie are not by Cocteau.[27]

Cocteau was well aware of the fact that had his ballet resorted to
traditional plots—one of the acrobat's falling in love with the Little
Girl, who would be killed by the jealous Chinaman, who in turn would
be killed by the acrobat's wife, or any other combination—it would
have been successful. The novel is always dangerous.

The startling originality of *Parade* went undetected for the most
part. Few noted the fact that this ballet combined four art forms
(poetry, music, painting, and dancing); that it used unheard-of objects
on stage, such as a bicycle; that the choreography stemmed directly
from daily life; that the costumes and decor possessed a boldness of
expression, a freshness of conception, and an explosive quality unknown in its time.

*Parade*'s debacle hurt Cocteau. He was not, however, alone in his
misery. Apollinaire experienced similar turmoil with his "surrealist"
play *Tirésias' Breasts,* which dealt with the realistic problem of female

emancipation. It opened at the Théâtre Renée Maubel on 24 June 1917 and was condemned as vulgar and in bad taste, as "crude symbolism." Most shocking of all were the insults leveled at it by the cubists. Juan Gris, in particular, considered it a direct attack on their artistic movement. For example, he said, the protagonist's dress was painted with an assortment of fruits and monkeys, her face was blue, a direct satire undoubtedly on Picasso's "Blue period" (1909–13). Certain lines, such as the following, also drew the cubists' wrath:

> We have learned at Montrouge
> That Monsieur Picasso
> Is creating a movable painting . . .

Apollinaire and Cocteau were both called upon to defend themselves in a mock trial staged by the cubists. The first indictment concerned Cocteau. Why had he used the word "rue" in the sense of "ruer" (to kick or to buck), rather than in its literal sense in the poem "Zèbre," which he wrote for the program of *Tirésias' Breasts*. The second charge: Apollinaire had intentionally satirized the cubists, and this was unpardonable. Such a verdict, in Apollinaire's case, particularly, seemed rather strange in view of the fact that he had always been the champion of the cubists. Indeed, he was a bit annoyed by this "punitive seance," but it passed.[28]

Actually, these were minor incidents that in no way marred the unusual friendships these young enthusiasts enjoyed. Yet they illustrate the great importance and the seriousness with which they took their art, the integrity and devotion they displayed toward each other. A few minutes after Picasso learned of Apollinaire's death from influenza on the day of the Armistice, he looked at himself in a mirror and drew what he saw. It was the last self-portrait he ever made. Cocteau felt an aching void at the loss of Apollinaire.

## *The Rooster and the Harlequin*

The most daring lesson in our epoch has been taught to us by Satie: to be simple.[29]

By 1918 Cocteau had grown greatly in depth, understanding, and strength of feeling and conviction. His critical faculties were very keen in the field of art and perhaps even sharper in the realm of music. He was well equipped to write *The Rooster and the Harlequin* (*Le Coq et l'arlequin,* 1919), a manifesto made up of a series of maxims, aphorisms, and statements relating to music. In this work, Cocteau takes a strong stand for French music. He is insistent: "I am asking for a French music from France."[30] He casts aside with gusto the "bastard" music such as "French-German" or "French-Russian," whether it be inspired by Mussorgsky, Stravinsky, or Wagner. At the same time, he disavows the French Saint-Saëns, and Debussy, who he said fell into the "Russian trap." And with the usual Cocteau humor, he declared that Debussy transposes "Claude Monet à la russe." He speaks out plainly in favor of a simple, clear music, like Satie's and indicates in general terms the aesthetics of "The Six."

Gide took umbrage with *The Rooster and the Harlequin.* Cocteau, in turn, accused Gide of reacting too strongly to his work because he felt himself to be losing his grip on French youth. Irate, Gide printed a letter in the *Nouvelle Revue Française.* He asked Cocteau to come and see him and read him the open letter that was destined for him.[31] Jacques Rivière, a friend of Gide and editor of the *Nouvelle Revue Française,* refused to print the reply Cocteau wrote after his meeting with Gide. *The Rooster and the Harlequin* caused strain in several of Cocteau's friendships. Stravinsky, for example, was deeply offended by this manifesto. In fact, their friendship was brought to a momentary end because of it.

Cocteau, however, though he had not intended any offense with his work, was satisfied with it. His ideas concerning music had been clarified as a result of this manifesto, and, furthermore, he had given Satie the acclaim he deserved. When asked to contribute a column to *Paris-Midi,* Cocteau accepted and continued to elaborate his ideas on music and art.

Cocteau's column in *Paris-Midi,* entitled "Carte-Blanche," was filled with praise for the new music and poetry. Several articles dealt appreciatively with the works of Arthur Honegger, Darius Milhaud, Germaine Taillefer, Francis Poulenc, and Louis Durey. They also expressed admiration for the exoticism of his poet-friend Blaise Cendrars, author of *Panama* (1919), among other works. Cocteau had interesting insights into Derain's paintings, which he believed had preceded those of the cubists; comments on Picasso's and Braque's innovations; and on Matisse's canvases, which Cocteau felt were neither profound nor disciplined.

For relaxation, there was a ground-floor atelier at the far end of an obscure court at 6 Rue Huygens, where Cocteau used to love to go. There, in a smoke-filled room, audiences would freeze in winter and suffocate in summer as they sat and shoved against one another, listening to music and poetic recitations. Cocteau, Apollinaire, Max Jacob, Pierre Reverdy, and many others would enter into the festivities by reciting their own works. On other nights, Cocteau, who played the drums, would go to the Gaya Bar on Rue Duphot and listen to the latest jazz imports, responding to these sensual rhythms with fervor and excitement.

It was a day like any other day in 1919. The doorbell rang in Cocteau's apartment. "A child is in the ante-room waiting for you," said the maid. Cocteau went to greet Raymond Radiguet. He was fifteen, but could have been taken for eighteen, as he sported a cane. He had been sent by Max Jacob, he said.

Cocteau knew instantaneously that his life was going to veer sharply from the ordinary.

# Chapter Three

# Retrenchment—A New Reality

## 1919–23

> Such is the role of poetry. It unveils, in the strict sense of the word. It lays bare, under a light which shakes off torpor, the surprising things which surround us and which our senses record mechanically. [1]

To the captivated Cocteau, Raymond Radiguet was handsome, slender, charming, and a burgeoning writer. To the average individual, however, this youth might not have been so alluring. He was nearsighted, refused to comb his hair, and was deeply introverted. Cocteau, however, was fired by the inner beauty of the boy and by his wisdom which was far beyond his years.

Raymond Radiguet was an original thinker and not one to be led or to follow the trends of his day. In this respect, he was very strong. As for Cocteau, he was literally swept off his feet by the steady self-assurance of what Cocteau termed Radiguet's "genius," his charisma. He was overwhelmed, as Verlaine had been when he met Rimbaud.

Radiguet's influence on Cocteau's literary development was enormous. Though very young, he had great insight into Cocteau's weaknesses and strengths. As a writer, he had his own very definite literary ideas and principles. He warned Cocteau against the turbid and confused conceptions with which poetry, the novel, and the theater were riddled at the time and against the present vogue of the "poètes maudits" whose sole interest seemed to be rebellion and negativism. He urged him to struggle toward "clarity," precision, and to be a spokesman for a new classicism.

To suggest to the extremely successful Cocteau that he turn his back on popularity, that he shun the title of "youth's spokesman and ideal" which he had earned, that he refuse to set the pace for new and ever more revolutionary and obscure styles as was now demanded of him, that he decline invitations to the elegant social functions of the day—was asking a great deal, indeed. Yet Radiguet convinced Cocteau of the necessity for retrenchment, study, and renewal. He also persuaded him to reject "modernism," automatic writing which had just come into vogue, and anything which smacked of a fad. It must be stressed here that to opt for a rational approach to the arts, for the classical method in the early 1920s, was tantamount to self-destruction; it was quasi-revolutionary.

But Radiguet was very much aware, as was Cocteau, that an asset carried to the extreme becomes a liability. Cocteau's enormous versatility and popularity were his worst enemies. Because things came to him easily, he had a tendency to spread himself too thin. *The Potomak* and *The Cape of Good Hope* were works in which Cocteau's growth and depth of perception were evident. But were he to keep up the frenetic activities so characteristic of his compulsive extroverted personality, superficiality and monotony must follow. Every now and then, therefore, goals had to be set, and depths reached. Cocteau was one of those creative writers who needed a mentor to give him direction, to help him take stock of himself, to prevent a splintering of his being.

## *Poetry, Plain-Chant,* and *The Professional Secret*

> My angel, let me frolic in this field;
> No eye sees me, tell me, will I betray you?[2]

The two volumes of verses *Poetry* (*Poésies,* 1920) and *Plain-Chant* (1923) that Cocteau wrote while under Radiguet's influence reveal new ideas and a purity of style—the fruit of retrenchment and the birth of a new reality.

*Poetry* is a collection of sixty-three poems in which Cocteau introduces a whole new set of topics, themes, and motifs: the clown, the circus, the sailor, water, the dancer, the angel, the flag, the handkerchief, the elevator, travel, love, the horrors of war, and the athlete. Though some of these images and subjects appeared in Cocteau's earlier works, they are used in a different manner in *Poetry*. The athlete, for example, to whom Cocteau had always been attracted, now becomes a symbol for the poet. Impressed by the strength of the man who controls every aspect of his body, whose muscles are forever trim, whose strength increases with exercise, he feels that the poet, in a similar fashion, must also keep active, must take time out for training in order to reassess his worth. A simple style with fewer ellipses, devoid of accoutrements, more classical perhaps in design and demonstrating at the same time greater depth and force, mark *Poetry* with quite striking aspects.

In the poem "Spain" ("Espagne"), for example, Cocteau takes a series of popular images, those usually associated with this country, plays with them in such a way as to very nearly construct a vast canvas in words. A fan, gold, velvet, ebony, bulls, a *corrida,* a man singing to the accompaniment of a guitar—all these pictures appear in various sections of the poem, lending drama and color to it. What Picasso, Braque, Léger, Delaunay, de Chirico had done on canvas, Cocteau was now accomplishing in poetry, though he was not the first to try. This technique consisted of breaking up concrete objects as one conceives of them rationally, representing them in their variegated roles, and destroying the intellectual concepts of time and space, thereby achieving simultaneity and actuality.

The "Ode to Picasso" ("L'Ode à Picasso") is a particularly significant poem. It is divided into two parts. The first section, "The Seated Man" ("L'Homme assis") looks upon Picasso as a trainer of muses, a searcher, a man illuminated by an inner fire, with spirit that runs wild in his veins; a harbinger of revelations and unheard-of relationships. In the second section, "The Muses" ("Les Muses"), Cocteau compares the artistic creation, the painting, to a fugue, a mathematical entity, the dice of a solitary player, a man in constant communion with gods and planets, a Guignol and guillotine—one who eats of the city of life: "The solitary one / eats the city."

Cocteau believed that the creative artist is one who understands nature's conflicts: good and evil, light and darkness; who feels at one with the objects he portrays on canvas as Picasso did with the guitar and mandoline when he painted "The Girl with the Mandoline" (1910), "The Accordionist" (1911), and "Ma Jolie" (1912). Indeed, time and spatial perspective, as we know of them, are lost to the greater painter or poet who achieves transpersonal depths in himself. But for the routine artist, effects are merely distorted as though reflected on a glass or mirror. There is, however, a penalty to be paid for greatness. In order to reach one's core, a prerequisite for superiority in any form, one must sever, at one time or another, relations with the mainstream of existence, live in a world apart, "Closed houses in all senses." Only there, can one make "Astonishing discoveries."[3] Artists are like the monks at Port-Royal in the seventeenth century ("Les Solitaires"), who lived isolated lives in order to devote their energies to deepening their vision of God. Cocteau also likened the artist to the clown who, though he performs before multitudes, remains utterly alone. It is interesting to note that Cocteau used the clown, an image so frequently rendered in oil by Picasso himself, to describe this artist whom he labeled "the Harlequin of Port-Royal."[4]

The theme of water plays a prominent role in this volume of poetry. In "Oceano Roof," a parody on Hugo's "Oceano Nox," he describes boats making their way through the night, sadly surging from port to port, merchants selling their wares, the many natives they meet on the way, and their return, with sadness in their hearts. "Spring in the Depths of the Sea" ("Le Printemps au fond de la mer") is a delightful prose poem describing the wonders of underwater life. Like a motion-picture camera, the poet takes the viewer to the various parts of the pool, to watch the colorful fanlike array of burgeoning plant life, to feel the rhythmic surge of the water and listen to the splashing noises that emanate from all directions.

Stirred by the warmth of the sun he idolizes, Cocteau in "Batterie," achieves a sensuality and a Gide-like fervor rarely found in his poetry:

> Sun, I adore you like the savages,
> flat on their stomachs on shore.
>
> Tan, salt my body;
> Rid me of my great pain.
>
> The noon time tree filled with night
> Spreads it at night next to him.

The poet is in love with everything: the circus, the clown, the heat, and the dynamism of all that lives. The force of the plastic images, the alliterations, and the violence reach a sweeping crescendo:

> Sun, Buffalo Bill, Barnum,
> you intoxicate better than opium.
>
> You are a clown, a toreador
> you have golden watch chains.

In the last poem of this series, "Handkerchief" ("Mouchoir"), Cocteau waves good-bye to adoring crowds and to familiar shores and

announces the long trip ahead of him. He will move forward and like
Rimbaud "without oars, without gasoline . . ." plunge into the expanded regions of the unconscious or irrational realms.

"Plain-Chant" is one of Cocteau's most lyrical poems. It revolves
around three themes: love, death, and poetic inspiration. "Plain-
Chant" tells the story of the poet's (Cocteau's) intense love for his angel
(Radiguet), his inner struggle with his muse, and his anguish at the
thought of death and the pain of parting with his beloved. The muse
talks to the poet, inspires him, injects him with feelings, and forces
him to create.

The angel, who can be considered the poet's unconscious as well as
his beloved, has become part of the poet's life-blood. The Angel who is
both physical and spiritual, guardian and mentor, divines the mysterious ways of the poet's world:

> You know what my mysterious path
> Is on your map,
> And as soon as I move away from it,
> You grab me by the hand.
>
> Angel of ice, of mint,
> Of snow, of fire, of ether,
> Heavy and light as air,
> Your gauntlet torments me.[5]

The poet is comforted by the angel and his muse. When death
approaches, the poet begins to know real terror. But with death as with
sleep, two worlds become visible, a second sight develops, and opaque
doors become transparent. When the muse withdraws, however, the
excruciating pain of intellectual sterility seizes the poet. Returning to
his angel for comfort, the poet experiences exquisite joy, and in terms
clearly reminiscent of the romantic era, he sings out his love, "May
such a great joy last forever."

The poet seeks to follow his Angel now, wherever he goes; whether
in the external world or within the world of dreams. Separation is no
longer bearable: "You're squeezing my body with your little strength /
Why aren't we plant, and with just one bark . . .[6] The thought of life
without his angel causes the poet to shudder, even a momentary separation is looked upon as disastrous. "I feel pain everywhere, except when I
am held in your arms." Other anxieties cascade forth. The poet is thirty

years old, and the angel is half his age. Should he leave the poet, death's "assassins" would clutch and crush him, and all the beauty and meaning of life would vanish.

Death, a theme which grows in importance as Cocteau's work evolves, is not always looked upon as evil or as the harbinger of pain. It can be beneficent, when considered symbolically, as a withdrawal from life, as a sinking into self, resulting in a surge of new ideas, feelings, and sensations, "Which dies when it must in order to be more fully alive." It was this kind of death that enabled Cocteau to write his classically metered "Plain-Chant." Rejecting his former frenetic life, he burrowed within and reached new depths of cognition, with beauty of form and classical restraint.

Cocteau had come a long way under the tutelage of Radiguet. His development is most marked in his critical essay *The Professional Secret* (*Le Secret professionnel,* 1922). Now his ideas have coalesced, his feelings concerning the arts in general have clarified, his point of view has become defined.

Cocteau declared in this work that Mme de Lafayette's novel *The Princess of Clèves* (1678), written in classical style and much admired by Radiguet, had become for him a model of what prose should be like: discerning, simple, detached, and bare of epithets, pessimism, and self-pitying attitudes.[7]

As for poetry, Cocteau declared in *The Professional Secret,* it is a twofold and conflicting process. The poet must search for purity, which requires a withdrawal from the world, while the need to express *reality* forces him toward society. To endure this opposition, to write truthfully requires a heroic attitude. Realism, as Cocteau understands it, does not include the "noble" or "learned" or "artificial" manner of proceeding as practiced by Flaubert. It is rather similar to the clear, concise, and objective attitude intrinsic to the works of Stendhal.

It is the function of the writer-poet, Cocteau continues, to infuse new force and meaning into worn words and associations.

Put a platitude in place, clean it, rub it down, shine it up in such a way as to have it radiate youth, that same freshness, that same jet stream quality that it had in the beginning, and you will create the work of a poet.

The rest is literature.[8]

Poetry should express states of being. It is a manifestation of the spiritual in man; that religious feeling, not limited to any set of dogmas, which is at the center of each person. The poet, therefore, is like the priest of old, the professor of secrets he must never divulge. If the mystery is revealed, he will lose his wonder-working power.

In *The Professional Secret*, Cocteau also expands upon that which he had merely touched upon in *The Discourse of the Great Sleep* and which will become an important principle in his art: *angelism*. The image of the angel in no way resembles the child's conception of this figure: a good and kind being who watches over man. Actually, Cocteau's angel is a projection of himself, a composite of opposites that pull and tug at each other, creating the tension that results in the work of art:

Distinterestedness, egoism, tender pity, cruelty, suffering upon contact, purity in debauchery, a mixture of a violent taste for the pleasures of the earth and a disdain for them, naïve amorality, do not be mistaken: these are the signs of what we call angelism, those which all true poets possess; whether they write, paint, sculpt or sing. Few people admit it, because few people feel poetry.[9]

Rimbaud was the perfect example of "this kind of angel on earth."

All true poets trudge the solitary and difficult road—as would Cocteau himself.

Because I am unable to become affiliated with any school, nor create one of my own; public opinion, enamored of labels, pins all of them on me. For this reason, I represent Dadaism in foreign countries when, in fact, I am the bête noir of the Dadaists.[10]

## *The Do-Nothing Bar* and *The Wedding on the Eiffel Tower*

I say "absurd" because, instead of attempting to keep this side of the absurdity of life, to lessen it, to organize and arrange it as we organize and arrange the story of an incident in which we played an unfavorable part, I accentuate it, I emphasize it, I try to paint *more truly than the truth*.[11]

Cocteau was searching for a new reality, a fresh vision of the world he could express in art, perhaps with the help of music.

Music had always played a vital role in his life. He often played American jazz with a pianist and a saxophonist at the Gaya Bar. Every week, he met with Darius Milhaud, Arthur Rubenstein, Georges

Auric, and other musicians. They would first dine, either in a restaurant in Montmartre or at the Madeleine, then proceed to Milhaud's apartment, where the rest of the evening would be spent either playing or talking about music.[12]

Cocteau had a novel idea. He wanted to write a pantomime or mimodrama to be called *The Do-Nothing Bar* (*Le Boeuf sur le toit*). He asked Darius Milhaud to compose the music and Raoul Dufy to design the sets and decor. The title for this work had been suggested to him by Paul Claudel who, during the course of his travels in South America, had seen this name on a sign in a café.

*The Do-Nothing Bar* opened at the Théâtre des Champs-Elysées on 21 February 1920 and created a furor. The action takes place in a speakeasy. There is a police raid, a bartender saves the situation by lowering the electric fan which decapitates a policeman, a woman celebrates this piece of good fortune by walking "on her hands like the Salomé of the Rouen Cathedral," the bartender puts the policeman's head back on his shoulders and gives him "a bill three yards long" for his troubles.

*The Do-Nothing Bar* was, needless to say, novel. The cardboard or papier-mâché heads designed by Dufy and worn by the actors were three times the size of those nature had bestowed upon them. They were a kind of slow-motion type movable decor that confronted the audience with a series of grotesque images. The general dehumanization of the characters in this work shocked the spectators, accustomed as they were to the well-made boulevard play with its identifiable characters upon whom they could easily project.

The famous Fratellini clowns mimed the text. The audience's attention was focused on their gestures and bodily movements, since their heads were hidden under Dufy's cardboard masks, emphasizing immediately the impersonal element of the work. Darius Milhaud's music, inspired by catchy Brazilian tangos, contributed additional color to the already bizarre and hypnotic scene. Moreover, Cocteau introduced rhythmic and sensual jazz to the stage in this mimodrama that underlined the variegated types included in it: a boxer, society people, beautiful girls, a dwarf, a book-maker, a bartender.

The powerfully negative response of the public to this work was a setback. Yet, interestingly, a bar opened in Paris shortly after the mimodrama's premiere, which became one of the most elegant and popular in the 1920s and 1930s, and it was named "The Do-Nothing Bar" ("Le Boeuf sur le toit").

Despite the failure of *The Do-Nothing Bar,* Cocteau's imagination could not be dampened. He was bursting with ideas. Another play, *The Wedding on the Eiffel Tower* (*Les Mariés de la Tour Eiffel*), opened on 18 June 1921 at the Théâtre des Champs-Elysées, and was performed by the Swedish Ballet, with music by "The Six," and costumes and sets by Jean and Valentine Hugo.

*The Wedding on the Eiffel Tower* is a plotless play (plotless in the sense that dreams are plotless). There are no climaxes, and there is no organic building of episode upon episode.

The action takes place on the Eiffel Tower. There are two main protagonists, Phono One and Phono Two. At the beginning of the play they announce the fact that an ostrich has just walked across the stage. Seconds later, a hunter rushes on stage chasing the ostrich. Instead of shooting the ostrich as is his intention, he shoots a telegram which has just dropped onto the stage. The noise awakens the director of the Eiffel Tower. He opens the telegram which announces the arrival of a couple who are to be married on the Eiffel Tower. Tables are made ready and the wedding party enters. The procession walks by "strutting like dogs in an animal act."[13] The photographer takes the usual wedding pictures, uttering the same words spoken at countless weddings, "Watch the birdie." A surprise. A child emerges from the camera. The photographer remarks that he looks just like the parents, the grandparents, and so on. Relatives discuss the child's future: "Will he be President of the Republic?" or "A beautiful little victim for the next war."[14] The child begins to rebel as does every adolescent. "I want to live my own life! I want to live my own life!" he screams.[15] During the action, the hunter returns still chasing the ostrich.

If the play's action were looked upon in a realistic manner, it would be considered absurd. A child, emerging from a camera? followed by a nude swimmer? then a lion devouring a general? A hunter chasing an ostrich on the Eiffel Tower? A child rebelling against his parents at the tender age of two or three? These occurrences, impossible in real life, can occur in the unconstrained dream world. In the expanded universe of the unconscious world, clock time is abolished: weddings, children, growth, future—all can occur at once and in color. In this attempt to extend the limited reality to which audiences had grown accustomed, Cocteau, like Apollinaire and Jarry before him, opened up a whole new realm where the impossible happens.

*The Wedding on the Eiffel Tower* is also a satire. The entire bourgeois wedding ceremony is mercilessly mocked in comments made about the bride and the groom: "rich as Croesus," "pretty as a heart." War, patriotism, and youth's usual rebellions are also parodied: "I want to live my life" cries the two-year-old.

There are no real characters in Cocteau's satiric work. Two actors, encased in boxes shaped in the form of phonographs with horns for mouths, are placed on either side of the stage. They are in many respects reminiscent of the ambulatory kiosks of Apollinaire's *The Breasts of Tirésias* (1917). These human phonographs, who comment on the action taking place on stage, remind one of the old Greek choruses, assuming the role of masters of ceremonies. To lend an even more unconventional note to the theatrical spectacle, Cocteau used a technique of Jarry's, specifying that his creatures must have a "special" tone of voice. The voices, therefore, emanating from the human phonographs were loud, emotionless, and very clear.

The text was a medley of commonplace phrases and routine words. Cocteau ridiculed hackneyed expressions and at the same time gave them new vitality because he used them with humor and originality. For example, the photographer says to the wedding party, "Don't move anyone, watch the birdie come out"; and an ostrich actually emerges from the camera—a platitude indeed, but this one walks!

The most striking innovation in the entire production, however, was the dissociation of speech and action, wherein the actor and the speaker were two different people. The human phonograph or narrators spoke all the lines, while the protagonists mimed and danced their parts. In this manner, conventional empathy—between audience and actor speaking his lines—was abolished. The actors expressed their emotions and thoughts physically, but never articulated them. Since there was no meaningful connection between the actor and the speaker, the words seemed hollow and devoid of meaning. The atmosphere created in theater was bizarre and unreal, leaving many in the audience irritated, if not downright angry.

The music composed by "The Six" added to the general excitement. The waltzes, marches, overtures, fugues, quadrilles, frequently derived from popular French folk songs, set the pace for this novel work. Cocteau believed he had created a new genre with *The Wedding on the Eiffel Tower*, which was neither ballet nor opera nor theater, strictly speaking, but a combination of the dance, acrobatics, mime, drama, satire, and the like.

In the Preface to *The Wedding on the Eiffel Tower* (written in 1922), Cocteau explicated his attitude toward the theater. He advocated a "poésie de théâtre" rather than a "poésie au théâtre," the discovery of new meanings in common everyday objects and topics. Cocteau favored an anti-naturalistic theater at a period when the well-made plays of the Boulevard theaters were the rage. His innovations, he hoped, would be as shocking as Antoine's had been when he founded the naturalistic Théâtre Libre in 1887. Audiences in that earlier time had been aghast when Antoine placed actual pieces of meat on the tables on stage, real-life props—all in order to increase audience credibility. But what had once been novel, Cocteau noted, was now commonplace. By 1922, spectators were discontented at a theatrical performance that did not feature real objects. Cocteau had no objection to real objects, provided they were used in a totally unconventional manner, as he had demonstrated in *The Wedding on the Eiffel Tower,* when two humans, encased in large boxes resembling phonographs, appeared on stage.

Cocteau in no way attempted to abolish reality *as he saw it.* Indeed, he refused to "attenuate" or "arrange" the "ridiculous" elements he encountered in life. On the contrary, he accentuated those very aspects, striving to portray a world which was "more truly real than the truth," as Ionesco would do years later. Cocteau insisted, rather, on a reality in depth. The two narrators in *The Wedding on the Eiffel Tower,* were brought out into the open, their thoughts and attitudes were aired. Nothing remained hidden. "I illuminate everything, I underline everything," Cocteau wrote. Man's inner world with all of its hideous and beautiful aspects must be laid bare.

A play for Cocteau must form a cohesive whole. It must be simple and orderly, direct and to the point. Ideally, it should be created by one individual, "a universal athlete," as he called him, who would be capable of writing, directing, decorating, costuming, and even acting and dancing the production. Since such a goal is almost impossible to realize, Cocteau felt that this "universal athlete" should be replaced by a "friendly group," which is exactly what the musicians, the poets, and the painters were who worked together on *The Wedding on the Eiffel Tower.*[16]

Irritated by the strange music, the discontinuity in the story line, and the broken boundaries of conventional reality, audiences did not respond in kind to the efforts of the "friendly group."

With the *Wedding on the Eiffel Tower,* I built right on the boards a great transmitting instrument for poetry. I pride myself on having displayed a poetry of the theatre for the first time; in the face of a total lack of comprehension, even on the part of admirers; for a poetry in the theatre is a mistake, a fine guipure seen from afar. My cord guipure remains misunderstood. They applauded a farce, a satire, nothing of what I had in mind. Because I have suppressed all images and all finesse of language. Only poetry remains. For modern ears, therefore, nothing is left. Anglo-Saxons consider *The Wedding* nonsense.[17]

## *The Great Split* and *The Impostor*

To be sufficiently acute, sufficiently rapid, to cross the droll and the painful in one fell swoop, this is what I am practicing to do.[18]

Cocteau's novel *The Great Split* (*Le Grand écart*, 1923) was just as unorthodox as *The Wedding on the Eiffel Tower*. The title of the book itself, *The Great Split,* is indicative of this work's subject, the traumatic battle a youth wages with himself as he passes from adolescence to maturity; from the protection and comfort offered to him by mother and home, to the world with all of its dangers and misfortunes. *The Great Split* is a description of the growth process really, of the young and handsome Jacques Forestier whose personality still has not coalesced and whose sexual demarcation is still unclarified.

Jacques Forestier, handsome, highly emotional, switching from moods of extreme joy to those of deathlike sorrow, feels unloved, rejected by women, babied by his bourgeois mother. He has reached a turning point. Returning to Paris from a trip to Venice with his mother, he prepares his baccalaureat examination. At the pension where he is staying, he meets the Oxford-educated Peter Stopwell, a champion jumper who resembles a Greek god. Jacques falls in love with a dancer, Germaine, the mistress of the rich Nestor Osiris. After a tempestuous liaison with Germaine, Jacques, whose ecstasy has known no bounds and whose life has been filled and colored by her, is jilted. Peter Stopwell finally wins Germaine's favors. Disconsolate, Jacques makes an abortive attempt at suicide. After a long convalescence, he finally begins to face life as a man.

Symbolically, Jacques's painful emergence into manhood is another way of describing the creative process every artist goes through at one time or another during his life. Cocteau depicts Jacques's journey into adulthood (the novice becoming an artist) by means of the characters themselves and also stylistically.

In *The Great Split,* the characters are all undeveloped. The hero is *split:* witty and serious, melancholy and humorous, elegant and sloppy, aristocratic and a man of the people, hard and soft, creative and sterile, hypocritical and sincere. Cocteau resorts to variations in color to further juxtapose the division intrinsic to Jacques's personality:

Half shadow, half light: this is the lighting of planets. Half of the world is in a state of repose, the other, at work. But from this half which dreams, there emanates a mysterious force. [19]

Not only is Jacques's character splintered, but so are all the other beings portrayed in this novel who are, in effect, projections of the central character. They are childlike, amoral, transparent, and disordered. There are no sexual or emotional gradations or distinctions, no profound relationships. Jacques has no rapport with his mother, who never once is looked upon as a person, but is referred to almost as a function. The father image is nonexistent: "If we erase Mr. Forestier, it's because he erased himself."[20] Jacques's relationship with Germaine is no more profound; the enormous passion he feels for her keeps him in a state of "paradise" which means, in effect, childhood (comfort-nonexistence). Such a feeling could not even be referred to as love, since it was nurtured neither by appreciation, admiration, or even affection. Jacques's passion simply invaded his life, and the ensuing pain left him with a need to escape into sleep or death.

The world of the unconscious which Jacques enters when asleep permits him to escape his sorrow:

It happens with man, that his slumbering half contradicts his active half. True nature rises and speaks. If the lesson is to be a profitable one, then let man listen and set his enlightened half in order; the shadow half will become dangerous. Its role will change. It will send up miasmas. We will see Jacques come to grips with this night of the human body. [21]

But the temporary surcease of sleep was not sufficient—so followed the abortive death try. One of the most arresting descriptions in the novel is Jacques's attempted suicide and the ensuing sensations:

The cold from the ethyl chloride vaporised his eyes and his cheeks. Waves of goose flesh overran all parts of his body and stopped about the heart which was beating to the bursting point. These waves, coming and going, from the toes to the roots of the hair, were imitating an all-too-short sea; which always removes from one beach what it gives to another. A mortal cold replaced the waves; it played, it spread, disappeared and reappeared, like designs on moire. [22]

After Jacques's brush with death, permanent withdrawal from reality is no longer possible. He therefore returns to life, reconciled to the necessity of struggle and to its beneficent aspects.

Cocteau's style is replete with images, humor, exoticism, metaphors, and similes. The images he uses are important in that they reveal certain aspects of his protagonists' personalities. Images such as glass, windowpanes, and mirrors have certain common qualities: they reflect, are brittle and hard, transparent to a certain degree, and thin. And like these objects Cocteau's creatures are continually looking about, gazing at each other directly or indirectly (a reflection of themselves), as though trapped in a Hall of Mirrors, unstable; their ceaseless activity leads them into a state of total confusion, rendering them incapable of finding any meaning in their lives. Frequently, they are confronted with their own utter emptiness; "Jacques was exhausting himself desiring the void."[23] As for Germaine, "Even if Germaine feels a caprice, she will encounter the void."[24] Furthermore, these creatures are all narcissistic and undeveloped. Unlike the Greek god who fell in love with his own image and was swallowed up by the waters when trying to make contact with himself, Jacques hates his own image. Though he is aware of the dichotomy within himself, he cannot accept what he considers to be his ugly, frail, and weak side. He wishes desperately to be objective, dispassionate, cerebral, and always in perfect control of himself.

Cocteau frequently uses the humor of jokes, puns, adjectives, and epithets in a provocative manner, to underline the irony and satire of certain situations. Germaine's lover was called, for example, Nestor Osiris and he was "so rich that his name alone spelled wealth."[25] As for Germaine's character, "Germaine's freshness came from dung. She fed on it with the gluttony of a rose . . ."[26] Humorous names describe personality traits: Mme Supplice, the concierge; Petit copain, the young and naïve boy who becomes Peter Stopwell's slave; Stopwell, given to a person who is conceited, arrogant, narcissistic, who sees his own image reflected in the water "which he succeeded in stopping."

Cocteau uses similes and metaphors to describe the inner being by means of an exterior object. Jacques's personality was so turbulent and confusing, it resembled, Cocteau wrote, the disorder of women's rooms:

Jacques' room resembled those unmade rooms of Montmartre women who get up at four o'clock, put a coat on over their night gowns, and then go down and get something to eat.[27]

Moods are also set in this manner. A sunset, for example, resembles a *corrida* because both are bloody and painful and both require intense courage and skill.

*The Great Split,* which is not necessarily autobiographical though it was written in that style, deals with an unhappy love affair and has been compared, perhaps for this reason, to Flaubert's *Sentimental Education.* What makes Cocteau's novel unique, however, is the manner in which the tale and themes are treated, the extreme objectivity of the style which gives the reader the impression that the entire work is nothing but a farce, and the fact that the characters (projections of the author) are like puppets—unfeeling, and wooden. Cocteau banished all sentimentality from his novel and also broke away completely from the traditional novel à la Balzac or Flaubert, with their analytical and psychological approach, their three-dimensional characters, their plot lines, and their naturalism. Cocteau's characters have no substance or depth, but like emanations or disembodied fantasies, they roam around the pages, fluid, unstable, and rootless, searching for something, somewhere. Cocteau's creatures in many ways anticipate the current new novel.

With *The Great Split,* Cocteau's reputation as a novelist was definitely secured.

Cocteau's next novel, *The Impostor (Thomas l'Imposteur,* 1923), was written with the steady hand of a master. It revolves around World War I and an adolescent's strange adventures during that confused period.

Guillaume Thomas is sixteen years old, the nephew of a concierge. At the start of World War I he is too young to serve, but nevertheless has visions of being a great hero. He steals a uniform, sews gold braid on the arms, enters a Red Cross center run by a Doctor Verne, offers his aid, and declares himself to be Guillaume Thomas de Fontenoy, nephew of the famous Commander General of the French troops. Everyone believes his fanciful imaginings and is captivated by his charm. He meets Henriette, the daughter of the Princess of Bormes and falls in and out of love with her. Because of his beguiling ways and his famous name, he obtains practically anything he wants, even certain papers permitting him to leave with a convoy for the front. At the front Guillaume is struck by a bullet, but is still unable to accept the reality of the situation and declares, "I must absolutely make believe I am dead, otherwise I am lost!" He dies. Henriette cannot stand the shock and she commits suicide.

Rather than draw realistic descriptions of certain battles or narrate political maneuvers that took place during World War I, Cocteau preferred to splash-paint his canvas with his characters' impressionistic reactions to give aspects of trench warfare, to the government's move from Paris to Bordeaux, to the Battle of the Marne, and to the description of the wounded. The very disparity between the tragedy of the true events and the flippant, always humorous manner in which they are recounted in *The Impostor,* not only leaves the reader with an indelible picture of what occurred, but with a real feeling of malaise.

In *The Impostor* the war is seen as a treacherous, selfishly motivated, ghastly joke. The confusion and disorganization brought on by war, for example, which is an outward manifestation of man's inner chaotic world, is described simply as "The war began in the greatest disorder. This disorder never ceased, from one end to the other."[28] In another image, the horrendous nature of war is compared to a theatrical spectacle, a "Theatre reserved to men." Human beings stand on the sidelines watching while uncontrolled emotions take the stage and enact the spectacle. The fanfare and excitement brought on by war are likened to the blood feelings of a bullfight: "The blood, the fever, the vertigo of bull fights did not attract him."[29]

A wide variety of characters appear on these pages: the candid Guillaume Thomas de Fontenoy, the egotistical medal-seeker Dr. Verne, the immoral Mme Bormes, and her daughter, the naïve Henriette.

Thomas Guillaume de Fontenoy, as he calls himself, is a charming, handsome young man who sails through life on a lie—which is actually his reality. He is not to be compared with Corneille's hero in *The Liar* (*Le Menteur*), who lied so much that no one believed him. Nor is he hypocritical or cunning, like Julien Sorel in *The Red and the Black.* He is, rather, naïve, sincere, in certain respects like Voltaire's Candide. Guillaume is unable to accept the reality of his life, which he considers uninteresting and perhaps even sordid; he rejects it entirely and lives only in the gamelike fairy-tale atmosphere of his fantasy.

Dr. Verne (perhaps a satire on Jules Verne) is an egoist, go-getter, interested only in his personal aggrandizement. His aim is to dominate everyone around him. And he does. He neglects his patients when it suits his purpose. Since his great desire in life is to obtain the military cross, "It guided him, like the star the Magi." He cultivates Guillaume because he believes him to be the nephew of the Commander of the French forces. Because of the image of the star and the Magi (likened to Christ and the Magi), Dr. Verne's obsession has an almost religious quality. In another vein, the author adds, "His cross turned before his eyes like artichokes in fire-works." Indeed, Dr. Verne's obsession with decorations is so intense that when he discovers Guillaume's true identity, he does not divulge it for fear that such a revelation might prevent him from receiving the cross.[30]

Mme Bormes, a Princess and Dr. Verne's friend, is a ludicrous creature. To point up her humorous and disparate attributes, Cocteau lists her various qualities and for a finishing touch, ends with a non sequitur: "Widowed very young from the prince, dead as a result from a hunting accident two years after their marriage, the Princess de Bormes was Polish."[31] Just as the sentence does not hold together, neither does her personality. She is amoral yet noble, pure though dissolute, sincere though hypocritical.

Henriette, her daughter, who falls in love with Guillaume, rapturously listens to him relate his adventure stories and delights in his every word. She is described succinctly as belonging to the race of listeners, of spectators of life. Henriette's love, though it alters her personality, is not dramatized nor do its meanderings keep the reader in a state of suspense. It simply makes her an instrument: "Love had turned Henriette into a Stradivarius, a barometer, sensitive to the least moral temperature changes." When Guillaume leaves for the front and is separated from Henriette, his passion grows by leaps and bounds, as the image of her becomes more and more unreal. Indeed, her reality finally disappears entirely, leaving her as nothing more than a figment of Guillaume's imagination: "She could enter into fiction." But as a fiction she exists powerfully. He can, therefore, play the part of an agonized lover, write her letter upon letter, tearing them all up as he finishes them. Henriette, however, never suspects the depth of his affection for her, which lasts only as long as she exists in his imagination alone. When he sees the real Henriette again, he promptly falls out of love with her: "He was in love with the batallion."

Guillaume's reactions vary according to the characters with whom he comes into contact. He is a chameleon and assumes a variety of personalities: the unfortunate, the innocent, the happy, the persecuted, whichever suits his fancy at that particular moment. Yet Cocteau describes him as "Guillaume, the artificial one, was without artifice." There is only one stable factor in his life—the basic lie which results from his inability to accept reality. Only once, when he is drunk, is he confronted with his true self and the world as others see it. At that moment "the fragile cover of reality" lifted and the real world intrudes into his make believe. The reverse would occur to an ordinary individual, alcohol releases the pent up emotions and permits fantasy to roam. Guillaume, however, lives in a world completely reversed from normality. He is, indeed, an original. Only at the end of the novel does the outside world finally come to accept Guillaume's inner world or his reality. After his death the following words are engraved on his tombstone: "G.-T de Fontenoy. Died for us." Fiction has become fact.

In this detached, unsentimental, yet fanciful "story," Cocteau makes use of certain literary devices to point up the humorous, ironic, and fairy-tale qualities so dear to him.

When irony is uppermost in Cocteau's mind, he describes an individual with one vibrant image, "The woman kissed his amethyst, the men awaited his orders. Handsome and swollen, he was a fabulous fuchsia . . ." To emphasize certain images, he endows them with an eternal quality by comparing them to various aspects of paintings by famous artists. Clouds, for example, are like the "whirlwind of angels" in a Murillo painting. In this manner, the reader is immediately impressed by the disorder, yet the purity, of such physical manifestations of inner contents. His description of wounded soldiers gains poignancy when he compares their coloring, their extreme thinness, and their gestures to El Greco's monks.

Metaphors and similes add to the dynamism of the novel. The development of the war, for example, is likened to the ripening of a fruit that falls from a tree. The satiric overtones of such an image are many; the triviality of the falling apple can have devastating effects, for example, as witnessed by the biblical story. Certain images are humorous because of their extravagant and outlandish nature. Mme Bormes's life is compared to the artistry of a piano virtuoso who "can draw all the effects possible that musicians draw from mediocre as well as beautiful compositions. Her duty was pleasure."[32] Images of an unpleasant nature are presented in a flippant manner and underline the horror of various situations. A wounded soldier, for example, who could no longer be operated upon, is described in the following manner: "They had to let gangrene invade him as ivy does a statue."[33]

Though Guillaume is shot at the end of the book he survives as a youthful, imaginative fellow in most of Cocteau's ensuing works. Whatever form he takes, he creates a whole cosmogony for himself: plays cruel or kind games, and functions as an individual, but only in his

own world, that of the poet who has not yet been able to leave the land
of childhood and adolescence, who suffers from a sorrowful affliction—
the dread of life.

In this postwar novel, Cocteau dramatizes the incompatibility between the inwardly focused life of the poet whose reality lies in his
imagination, and the rational and prosaic life of the man who lives in
the workaday world. If Guillaume, the charming, naïve poet is to
survive at all in the world, he must be allowed to relate in his own way
to the outside world that, in turn, must respond to him on his terms.

The word *impostor* in Cocteau's *The Imposter,* is a metaphor for the
creative individual: the poet or the artist who is also the child. Cocteau
noted in his novel:

You will see what kind of an impostor Guillaume was. His sort are a race
apart. They live halfway between reality and make believe. They are distinguished, not lowered, by the deception which they practice. Guillaume took
people in without malice. The story will show that he took himself in. Like
any child, cabby or horse, he forgot what he really was.[34]

## Chapter Four
# Pain Killers
### 1923–28

My laziness loves to take orders. From whom would I consent to receive orders, if not from God? Mysticism is not what convinced me. I adore miracles, but they bother me really as do all proofs. What convinces an undecided intelligence is the carcass of our religion: its numbers, its algebra of love.[1]

Radiguet's death shattered Cocteau. He felt broken in body and in mind. He was hardly recognizable.

After months of despair he was persuaded by Diaghilev to come to Monte Carlo with him. There, he could rest and watch the Russian impresario at work, rehearsing Francis Poulenc's *Les Biches* and Georges Auric's *Les Fâcheux*. The hope, of course, was that he would be stimulated to write something. Once in Monte Carlo, however, Cocteau met Louis Laloy, the administrator of the Opera House, author of a book on opium. Aware of the poet's extreme despair, Laloy introduced him to the drug. Cocteau took to it as a dog to water after having been lost in the desert.

Cocteau now began living in the past, recalling the days of joy he had known with Radiguet, the amount of work he was able to do. He remembered particularly his free adaptation of Sophocles' *Antigone,* which had opened nearly a year before Radiguet's death, 19 December 1922. He had always felt a particular affinity for Greek theater, with its sense of mystery and awe, its religious and ritualistic aspects.

*Antigone* had been very successful, with costumes designed by Coco Chanel, sets created by Picasso, and music composed by Honegger. Cocteau had synthesized this ancient drama, reducing the chorus to one individual. He had modernized the language by introducing colloquialisms at the same time, injecting into it a strange musicality that lent a supernatural aura to the entire production. The cast too was exciting: Cocteau was the one-man chorus, the young Antonin Artaud now in his prime acted the blind Tiresias, Charles Dullin was Creon, and the hauntingly beautiful Genica Athanasiou was the fiery Antigone. The play lasted forty minutes. In that short period a tremendous empathy had been created between audience and protagonists. On one occasion, in fact, Cocteau had heard a female spectator scream out, as Antigone was being led to her death, "But . . . she was not guilty."[2] In general, critics had been favorably disposed to Cocteau's adaptation. They commented on the poetic quality of the lines and the verve with which the actors had performed. André Gide was one of the very few who voiced contempt for *Antigone*. He referred to it as "Sophocles' play by Cocteau" and considered it "beautiful despite Cocteau" rather than because of him.[3] As was to be expected, the strict classicists objected to any tampering with great works. They considered Cocteau's rendition presumptuous and unwarranted. No matter, thought Cocteau. *Antigone* was performed two hundred times, a record for that era. Years later, however, he wondered whether this stroke of good fortune had not been in part due to the fact that Pirandello's play *Voluptuousness of Honor,* which had received triumphant criticism, was given on the same program.

The production of *Antigone* seemed very far away from Cocteau at this point, almost a pleasant dream. Now, he was apathetic, devoid of energy and direction. Though opium dulled his pain somewhat, it had not inspired him to pursue his career. Even when Count Etienne de Beaumont suggested a production of Cocteau's adaptation of *Romeo and Juliet,* entailing little effort on the poet's part since he had completed this text in 1916, he accepted the proposal only halfheartedly.

*Romeo and Juliet* opened on 2 June 1924 at the Cigale Theatre. Cocteau, prevailed upon to play the part of Mercutio, was like a deadweight. His friends had to literally push him on to the stage and after his lines were spoken, he walked off crying uncontrollably. Cocteau was exhausted. He could not sleep an night, yet slept standing up at the most unlikely places. He ate little and looked "like an insect" with a "carapace" for a costume.[4]

Whatever projects Cocteau undertook at this juncture seemed devoid of any real interest for him. Still on opium, he began to show signs of ill-health. He needed relaxation, good food, and the possibility of healing his torn self. The Hotel Welcome at Villefranche-sur-Mer had been suggested to him. This charming hotel, the fairy-tale atmosphere of the warm and aesthetically exciting town, helped Cocteau to the road to recovery. As the days passed, he felt a certain amount of incentive return, slowly, at first, then more rapidly.

Cocteau had become anxious to return to the source of drama—to Greece. He wanted to adapt another tragedy. The Theban legends had always been a source of fascination for him, *Oedipus Rex* especially. Each time he read this tragedy his whole childhood came alive for him. He remembered every detail of the performances given by Mounet-Sully at the Comédie Française, how this lionesque Oedipus struggled on stage amid the animal-like sounds that emanated from his mouth. These vivid memories acted as a stimulant for Cocteau. He began to work on a free adaptation of his own.[5]

Cocteau reduced the five-act *Oedipus Rex* to one act. He shrouded the atmosphere of the drama with a feeling of disaster from the very outset. Indeed, he even warned audiences not to expect the usual "pure" conception of a "divine" Greece. They would be exposed to a "ferocious" land inhabited by cruel gods who devoured each other and whose aims were to "ensnare human beings."

Cocteau completed *Oedipus Rex* at Villefranche-sur-Mer on 27 October 1925. And though this play was not produced until 1937, it served, along with *Antigone,* to usher in a new mode: the adaptation and modernization of classical tragedies. André Gide and Jean Giraudoux soon followed his example. Indeed, when Gide adapted Oedipus years later, he uttered one of his typical witticisms to Cocteau when he said, a veritable "oedipémie" is taking place.

## *Opéra*

The most must be taken like an aspirin.[6]

Despite his gradual recovery, Cocteau's opium intake had not diminished. His friends prevailed upon him to enter the Thermes Urbains Sanatorium in Paris to try to rid himself of the opium habit. The Thomist philosopher Jacques Maritain visited him there and spent many hours trying to convince him that a return to Catholicism would lift his depression and bring him new life. Cocteau accepted Maritain's help. When he left the Sanitorium he visited Maritain at his home in Meudon where he was introduced to Father Charles Henrion. Deeply impressed by this priest, Cocteau began taking religious instruction from him, and received the sacraments at his hands. A return to religion, at least for a while, gave him strength and a sense of belonging.

Life now had boundaries, order, direction, and most important of all—a future.

Radiant and renewed, Cocteau returned to Villefranche. There, he met the artist Christian Bérard who was to become very important in his future theatrical life. For the first time since Radiguet's death Cocteau felt capable of articulating his anguish. He turned to what had always been closest to him—poetry. In the slim volume of verses entitled *Opéra* (1925), a group of fervent, chantlike poems, he expressed his grief with restraint, detachment, and artistry.

*Opéra* is the poetic transportation of the many nuances of feeling he experienced when bereft of his love. Certain verses are detailed depictions of his opium fantasies, and these lend a haunting and almost frightening quality to the entire work. Other poems, relating the pain he felt in his most lucid moments, are replete with images drawn with the precision and surety of a Phidias or a Praxiteles. Cocteau's poetic credo, as revealed in *Opéra,* is still one of detachment, which he takes to be a prerequisite for creative art.

The poems devoted to Cocteau's opium fantasies ("By Himself" and "I Fly in Dream") are chiseled in incisive strokes. The feelings of lightness and giddiness are conveyed in harmonious tonalities, a blend of sharp consonants and free-flowing vowels, very nearly concretizing his drug-induced euphoria. During these periods he seemed to attain a kind of second sight that enabled him to discern the invisible from the visible, the inhuman from the human, and to express these visions in dramatic and poignant terms.

In "Mutilated Prayer" ("Prière mutilée") angels, glaciers, stars, and transfigurations of strange, haunting shapes all come into focus. In this poem the author seeks to do away with the realm of matter, in the platonic sense, which he finds so constricting and stultifying. He opts for the heavenly realm of the spirit, God's domain. There, he longs to ascend to those weightless regions depicted in somewhat similar terms by Victor Hugo in his poem "Ibo." In "Mutilated Prayer," the poet confronts the mysterious cosmic forces, watches the angels as they climb the mountains, and within him, he feels a divine presence. He demands to be charmed, loved, and cared for by God, refusing voyages, theater, and all the artifices of life on earth:

> I look at you for the last time from the wings,
> Scarecrow of the cherry-wood projectors.[7]

Such an inundation of strength as comes with the *numinosum* makes it possible for the poet to pursue his struggle to create. A struggle that requires continuous confrontation with forces beyond his control.

In "Light Prairie" ("Prairie Légère"), the poet again describes his mental flights, the exhilaration opium has given him, the thrill of celestial silence, of goalless glories, and the crushing sadness that follows at the heels of euphoria:

> I possessed the arteries' celestial tree.
> Silence is music with bamboo flutes,
> But Chinese hangmen want to silence me
> And caress death to seek the end.[8]

The shocking and ugly image of leprosy is used in "The Red Package" ("Le Paquet rouge"). This disease is turned into a metaphor to describe the inner disintegration that happens to the poet during his bouts with despair:

I am a leper. Do you recognize these moldy spots which simulate a profile. I do not know what charm my leprosy holds for the world, fools it and authorises it to kiss me.[9]

The poet wonders why the world is interested in him in view of his ugliness. Slowly, he discloses the fact that he reveals only that aspect of himself which he chooses to display: at times, the gruesome, tortured, leper-eaten side of his soul, at other moments, his elegant, beautiful self. There is no solution to the poet's suffering, he is a paradox—"I am a lie who always speaks the truth."[10]

In other poems, Cocteau uses whole series of images (glass, quartz, ice) to express the shallowness and pain of existence. These hard and cutting images convey to the reader a real feeling of physical suffering. At other instances, like De Quincey and Baudelaire, Cocteau describes a series of visions that seem to have emerged directly and intact from his childhood: snow statues[11] melting before the viewer's eyes, sleeping forms that reveal themselves to the dreamer, an array of strange relationships:

> The arteries, by the veins,
> Are rooted to the dream
> A man sleeping on the ground.[12]

"The Angel Heurtebise" ("L'Ange Heurtebise")[13] is the most important and complex poem of the series. Cocteau again takes up the
question of *angelism,* which he had defined in terms of an artistic
formula in *Professional Secret,* that is, the poet must be self-sufficient; he
must be emotionally and intellectually detached from the world. Rimbaud, he felt, best exemplified his credo because he had experienced life
to the hilt, had withdrawn from it when he willed to do so, and
relatively unscathed.

Cocteau personifies his angel in this poem and names him Heurtebise. He had come upon this strange name one day when visiting
Picasso on Rue la Boétie. As he was riding up in the elevator, he felt
himself getting bigger and bigger, overcome by a strange sensation.
Then he heard a voice screaming, "My name is on the plate," and
Cocteau read the sign on the elevator; "Elevator Heurtebise." For seven
days, Cocteau confesses, this name lived within him in the form of an
angel, it possessed him until "The seventh day . . . the Angel
Heurtebise became a poem and delivered me."[14]

In Cocteau's poem, the winged Heurtebise stands on a high step,
alone, the professor of supernatural powers. The earthly poet, on the
other hand, leads a constricted existence. He is dependent upon matter
and so knows only a limited universe. He calls to the angel, implores
him to help him out of his turmoil, to fill the void in his existence. But
Heurtebise, it is now revealed, has died. Like the young Greek gods,
however, he dies not once, but monthly, killed by God's angels. The
twelfth stanza, a highly melodious passage, reminiscent in this respect
of Hugo's "Les Djinns," is made up of a series of repeated words and
sounds, lending the entire verse an incantatory quality:

> Angel Heurtebise's death
> Was the death of the angel, Death
> Heurtebise was the death of the angel,
> A death of the Angel Heurtebise
> A mystery of change, an ace
> Which is lacking in the game. . . .[15]

As the poet searches about among the various aspects of his domain,
he realizes that he is utterly alone. He is chagrined. But he is not
totally solitary since "Cégeste," spelled phonetically (*ses gestes*), which
means "his gestures," has been sent to him. Cégeste, because of his
name, has come to mean a mirror image, perhaps of Heurtebise.

Though Cégeste is merely a replica of the true angel, he can still act as a kind of guardian to the poor poet who will have to be satisfied with the replacement and endure his earthly perigrinations stoically: unmoved, unaffected, and if possible untouched.

In *Opéra,* Cocteau uses both Christian and pagan symbolism, drawing from each that which he needs. His finely chiseled verses with their assonances and repetitions, take on an almost three-dimensional aura; though the images are abstract, they become palpable, acting entities, are of and yet removed from the land of the living. Like the poet in "Angel Heurtebise," Cocteau navigates free between inner and outer reality, emerging intact, with keener sight and sensibilities that, in turn, permit him to penetrate more deeply into even greater mysteries.

Indeed, the more Cocteau succeeded in expressing himself on paper, the stronger he felt, and the less dependent on Maritain and his Thomist Catholicism. In his extreme despair, it had appealed to Cocteau for several reasons: it reminded him of the religion of his childhood, when it had been a source of comfort, security, and joy; it appealed to him aesthetically, yielding a whole new series of beautiful images; and emotionally it had brought healing to the terrible wound caused by Radiguet's disappearance.

Sturdier now, Cocteau realized that he could never really subscribe to the Catholic dogmas of Jacques Maritain and his group—Henri Ghéon, Jacques Copeau, Francis Jammes, and Pierre Reverdy. In a letter to Maritain written from Villefranche-sur-Mer in October 1925 (published in 1926), Cocteau states his position quite clearly. He calls Maritain "a fish of great depths" with both his "luminous" and his "blind" spots.

Cocteau looked upon Maritain as a helpful and warming influence, a man of extreme kindness and understanding. He attributes Maritain's blindness to the fact that he was not able to see what Catholicism meant to the poet, the part it had and would come to play in the future in his life. Cocteau confesses that he has a deeply religious nature, which is manifested in his attraction to the unfathomable aspects in the cosmos. Such spiritual leanings, however, do not in any way presuppose a belief in dogma. He acknowledges, however, that his rapprochement with Catholicism has certainly helped him to understand better the meaning of his own inclinations, that it has given him the courage necessary to reveal himself *as he is,* anxieties, preoccupations, and pleasures.

In his letter to Maritain, Cocteau recapitulates the various stages in his life. There is a brief discussion of *Parade,* of the months spent at

Piquey with Radiguet, at Villefranche-sur-Mer with its easy "routine,"
the death of seven of his close friends (Garros, Radiguet, and others).
As for Radiguet, Cocteau explains, he realized too late that God had
only lent this "angel" to him for a short time. He uses the symbol of the
"glove" ("gant du ciel") to describe Radiguet's earthly clothing, a pro-
tective measure on God's part to prevent the youth from sullying
himself through contact with mortals. When heaven withdrew its hand
from the glove, it indicated Radiguet's death—or termination of his
earthly phase of existence. But death means only a separation; Radiguet
lives on as an angel.

Cocteau describes his own descent into hell in this same letter, his
use of opium, the influence of Father Charles Henrion, a pure soul who
knew better than anyone else, even after he had given him communion,
that Cocteau could not possibly remain in the fold. Father Charles
Henrion had discerned Cocteau's restless spirit, his active imagination
that could not be confined by fixed rules and precepts. For this reason,
he had told Cocteau, "Remain free." Maritain had been blind to this.

Cocteau remained a religious man, but not a practicing Catholic. He
felt himself to be far too aware of the limitations of organized religion
to continue adherence to it: "I shall learn that art is religion and will
show the danger of religious art."[16]

## Orpheus

Don't be deluded; this Orpheus is nothing more than a meditation upon
death.[17]

For years—ever since 1920—Cocteau had been intrigued by the
Orpheus myth and had wanted to write a play based on this subject. At
that time he had conceived of a five-act play, but when it was finally
completed in 1925 it was reduced to one act divided into thirteen
scenes. Originally also, Cocteau had thought of blending both Christian and Greek lore, weaving the Orpheus myth about the story of the
Incarnation: Mary, Joseph, and the angel. Such a plot Cocteau now felt
would certainly be misunderstood and misinterpreted and would un-
questionably cause a scandal. He did not have the strength now for the
fight such a work would entail. He opted, therefore, for a simpler
interpretation of the ancient Orpheus myth that would be novel
enough, he mused. In Cocteau's nimble fingers, the tragic Greek tale

became a humorous, yet disturbing drama, centering not about a heavenly couple, but rather on an "infernal ménage." The play, replete with puns and witticisms, introduced viewers into a magical and mysterious world of cleverly manipulated symbolism and imagery.

*Orpheus* opens with a modern apartment. A contemporary Orpheus and Euridyce are talking. Eurydice is a grasping wife, jealous of Orpheus' love for poetry and his "peculiar" attachment to a horse's head that has been placed in a circus box on stage. It is this animal that reveals the sentence, "Madame Eurydice will return from Hades" to Orpheus, and that he hopes to immortalize by submitting it to a poetry contest in Thrace. Orpheus leaves the apartment in a huff. He accuses Eurydice of nagging him, of smashing windows just to attract the attention of the glazier, Heurtebise. To continue the pattern, Orpheus smashes a window before leaving. Heurtebise arrives. He has brought a lump of poisoned sugar to feed Orpheus' horse; also an envelope from Aglaonice, Eurydice's best friend, a Bachhante whom Orpheus despises. After placing a letter in the envelope given her by Heurtebise, Eurydice seals it and dies moments later from the poison placed on it by Aglaonice. Death now enters the apartment dressed as a woman wearing rubber gloves. She is followed by two aids in surgeon's uniforms. Death gives the horse the poisoned sugar, performs a series of rituals, then exits. Heurtebise and Orpheus re-enter. Heurtebise shows Orpheus how to penetrate the land of the dead and join Eurydice. Orpheus puts on the rubber gloves Death had left by mistake, and steps into the mirror, then into Hades: "Mirrors are the doors through which Death comes and goes."[18] Moments later, Orpheus returns with Eurydice. She has been granted permission to remain on earth so long as Orpheus does not look at her. No sooner does she return, however, than their spats begin again. Orpheus inadvertently looks at her. She dies, Orpheus, seemingly unmoved, opens a letter left by the postman during his absence. It advises him to leave immediately; the Bacchantes are coming in a fury. They consider the poem he submitted to their contest a mockery. Orpheus, however, wants to resist the Bacchantes and defend his ideas. He goes out onto the balcony to speak, is stoned, and is then torn to pieces. His head appears on stage and then disappears. In the last scene, Eurydice and Orpheus, led by Heurtebise, are reborn. They go to their new house, having forgotten their past existence.

Cocteau dramatizes three themes in Orpheus: the conflict between the male and the female principles in the universe, the source of poetic inspiration, and an explanation of death.

To the ancients the Orpheus and Eurydice legend was more than a simple recounting of a love story; it represented a greater struggle between two forces in the universe, the solar (male) and the lunar (female) principles in religious worship. Aglaonice, a representative of the latter, was a sorceress and leader of the Bacchantes. She was determined to draw Eurydice into her group in order to strengthen the dark cult of Hecate that she represented. Her priestess performed voluptuous rites, attracting men into their fold and then forcing them to succumb, to admit the mastery of women over men. If they refused to do so, they were torn to pieces. Orpheus represented the male principle of the sun worshiper; he battled with these women, but died a horrendous death at their hands. [19]

Cocteau was not only fascinated by this basic struggle between two opposing principles that existed impersonally on a universal scale, but since he experienced this same struggle within himself, he related to it on a personal level. For example, Cocteau had never been able to relate to women in a normal male fashion in actual life. Such maladjustment is obvious in his novels *The Great Split* and *Thomas the Impostor,* wherein the women are ciphers at best. Indeed, Cocteau looked upon women in general as aggressive, possessive, and jealous. His Eurydice is an incarnation of this type. Instead of the loving, sensitive, and retiring girl of Greek tradition, Parisian audiences were presented with a devouring, material, and instinctual force of nature. Eurydice, unable to fathom poetry in general, jealous and distrustful of her husband's interest in art, as symbolized by the horse's head, is a harrowing termagant à la Albee.

Aglaonice and her companion Bacchantes are also *vagina dentata* types, murderous and destructive. The Bacchantes who tore Orpheus to pieces in the ancient legend are equally vicious in Cocteau's interpretation. They cannot understand poetry of any kind because they are women first and foremost, and so devoid of all sensitivity, bent upon one thing—the destruction of the male. They also represent tradition and the populace. They are the equivalent of the audiences that derided all of Cocteau's early efforts, that mocked the endeavors of the dadaists and the early surrealists, and, for that matter, that excoriated any new artistic movement throughout the ages. Orpheus, the gentle poet, the male-spiritual counterpart, could not possibly escape from the clutches of these horrendous women, except in Cocteau's fairy-tale end, when he is reborn.

The question of poetic inspiration is another theme in this drama.

Orpheus, both priest and man, was the legendary father of poetry and music, the possessor of a seven-stringed lyre that supposedly corresponded to the various moods of the soul. Since those practicing the Orphic cult believed in the magic power of language, it was said that Orpheus' songs and poems mesmerized everything and everyone with whom they came into contact: animal, mineral, vegetable.

For Cocteau, Orpheus was a modern poet in search of inspiration. As a poet, however, he is part priest and must, therefore, devote *all* his efforts and attention to his art, which is his religion. His marriage, however, fatally diverts his "fire" (energy). His dependence upon his steed Pegasus, looked upon by the Greeks as a symbol for poetic inspiration, increased as his own life became more and more unbearable. But let us not forget that Cocteau's Pegasus is not the fiery steed of antiquity, that powerful and gorgeously muscular animal. It has been reduced by Cocteau to a horse's head placed in a circus box. Such a conception of poetic inspiration indicates a humorous and satiric intent, also a word of counsel; inspiration can frequently play tricks on an unsuspecting poet; discernment and judgment, therefore, must always accompany any creative effort. The naïve Orpheus lacks this discrimination and accepts at face value the dictates of his horse, "Madame Eurydice will return from Hades," which he considered a truly great verse.

To declare, as Cocteau had time and time again, in the *Discourse on the Great Sleep* in particular, that poetry should not be merely transcribed of an arcane message and that mental faculties must be applied to verse in order to sift the wheat from the chaff—shocked and angered the avant-garde of his day—1925. André Breton, who had published his first *Surrealist Manifesto* just a year before, was incensed. He and his group had declared just the opposite point of view. They advocated automatic writing, spontaneity to the extreme. They believed that the messages coming to the conscious mind straight from the unconscious should not be altered in any way. One can readily understand why Cocteau became anathema to the surrealists.

Poets are also possessed of heroic qualities, according to Cocteau. They are martyrs of sorts, and Orpheus was no exception. Since he intended to fight the female and to hold fast to his point of view, against the exigencies of fate and life, he must suffer the fate of other such god-men: dismemberment and rebirth (Osiris, Dionysos, Christ).

Cocteau introduces a new character into the Orpheus legend, Heurtebise, the glazier, his guardian angel. Heurtebise, as we have already learned, had a very special meaning for Cocteau. He represented in part Radiguet's spirit and also a neuter force, the harbinger of both good and evil. In *Orpheus* he is the unwitting messenger of the evil Bacchantes, the plaything of superior forces, and the inadvertent killer of Eurydice. But this winged angel is also a good force: it is he who discloses to Orpheus the means of passage from one world to the next; it is he who leads Orpheus and Eurydice to their new home in the last scene.[20] He is, actually, a deus ex machina, a presence without whom the drama could never unfold.

Clearly, the Orpheus legend also serves to explain Cocteau's feelings concerning death. For the ancients, death was an initiation each person must experience before passing into another realm of existence . . . to rebirth. The Orpheus myth, a Hellenization of the Osiris cycle, taught the necessity of purifying the soul through expiation and religious consecration.

Cocteau retains certain of these ancient beliefs. For this reason, despite the humor and the irony in the play, there is always the element of mystery and a sense of the supernatural. Cocteau considers life a temporary state; a passage way toward another realm. To pass from one state to the next, however, requires passage through certain actual ordeals, after which secrets are revealed to the initiate. In *Orpheus,* Death is personified by Cocteau in the same manner as were religious figures during the Middle Ages—to render dogma plausible.

Death in *Orpheus* takes the form of a woman, since she is a procreating power and it is through her (Death), that rebirth can occur. She wears rubber gloves and operates with two aides, dressed in surgeon's uniforms. She is thus a twentieth-century figure. In this connection, one may recall Cocteau's letter to Maritain, in which he makes mention of Radiguet as an angel clothed "in gloves," to prevent any contamination through contact with the world of mortals or matter. The rituals enacted by Death and her two aides, in this drama have, undoubtedly, ironic overtones. Yet, these very rituals captivate Cocteau. They possess the same magical powers as any other religious ceremonies: prayers, rosary saying, incantations, and the like. They all have hypnotic overtones that ease the believer's way into another plane of existence.

Theatrically speaking, *Orpheus* is an exciting work. Objects become ritualistic symbols, virtual protagonists. Divested of their customary functions, these objects (doors, mirrors, gloves, glass) acquire new and startling meanings. Gloves are not merely used to keep hands warm or for reasons of fashion; they become mysterious entities. When worn by

Death, they give audiences the impression of witnessing an actual
operation. Later, they seem to turn into religious talismans, endowed
with the power to ensure safe passage from one world to the next:
"With these gloves you'll pass through mirrors as through water."
Mirrors likewise assume a different function. Habitually, they reflect
man's image, permitting him to indulge his narcissistic bent. In Cocteau's *Orpheus,* however, the mirror becomes an instrument by which
one sees Death's daily work: "You only have to watch yourself all your
life in a mirror and you'll see Death at work like bees in a glass hive."[21]
In this mirror, man faces his own aging and decaying self as does
Dorian Gray in the painting and Raphael Valentin in the shrinking
magic skin. Cocteau's mirror, like Alice's looking glass, becomes a
door that leads to the other world—life's counterpart. It is a mysterious
and magical instrument.

Endowed with new functions and powers, objects created a feeling of
uneasiness among the spectators. "Even familiar objects," Cocteau
wrote in his preface, "have something suspicious about them." In this
respect, Cocteau was a precursor of the "absurd" dramatists, like Ionesco, for example, whose plays frequently center on an agglomeration
of objects.

Cocteau introduces another interesting technique to his drama: he
purposefully breaks the audience-actor empathy. For example, after
Orpheus has died and his head remains on stage, the audience is not
only shocked but disconcerted when the head reveals his identity; it
declares itself to be Jean Cocteau and gives his address. Strangely
enough, the destruction of the theatrical illusion serves to reinforce it
still further. The audience's identification goes beyond the play's characters, to the author himself; the spectators have become the dramatist's
accomplices and are not permitted to share in his secrets and his jokes.
They are participating members of an arcane club.

Some strange coincidences occurred during the rehearsals of *Orpheus*—
so unusual in fact, that they bear repeating here. One day, as Cocteau and
the cast were rehearsing at his apartment, a loud noise was heard just as
the actor pronounced the line, "With these gloves you will pass through
mirrors as if they were water." The actors ran to the source of the noise,
the bathroom, only to discover that the mirror had shattered at that very
moment. In Mexico, when *Orpheus* was performed in 1926, an earth-
quake interrupted the Bacchante scene, demolishing the theater and
injuring several people. When the theater was rebuilt and *Orpheus* was

again scheduled, the performance had to be stopped because the actor playing the part of Orpheus was unable to exit from the mirror; he had died while performing.[22]

*Orpheus* opened in Paris on 17 June 1926 at the Théâtre des Arts. With George and Ludmilla Pitoeff playing the lead roles, it was an electrifying performance. The theater was filled to capacity with poets, painters, and musicians—le tout Paris. Many first-nighters, however, were stunned. They could not make out the play. Was it a comedy because of the puns, jokes, and innuendoes? A tragedy, since two people died? They questioned the meaning of the personification of Death, the unorthodox use of objects, the dehumanized and ambiguous nature of the protagonists, the symbols and the atmosphere of magic and mystery that pervaded. They had lost solid footing and were sliding into a new world where all established concepts and values either were questioned or, indeed, were no longer valid. It is no wonder then that many were flooded with a feeling of malaise.

## Oedipus Rex

Cocteau returned to Villefranche-sur-Mer shortly after the opening. There, he got in touch with Stravinsky, who lived with his wife and sons at nearby Mont-Boron. They made up the seven-year-old quarrel that had arisen as a result of Cocteau's outspoken manifesto, *The Rooster and the Harlequin.*

Stravinsky, extremely impressed by Cocteau's adaptation of Sophocles' *Antigone,* asked him to write an oratorio in Latin on *Oedipus Rex.* Cocteau was pleased with the proposition and was aware of the fact that Latin was the language of the ritual par excellence. He began working on it almost immediately and gave his vision to Jean Danielou to translate into Latin.

As reworked by Cocteau, *Oedipus Rex* included two acts and six episodes. Its classical simplicity, people suggested, had resulted from Cocteau's interest in the *Noh* drama. But Cocteau denied the influence, denying merely that he wanted to create as forceful and dynamic a work as possible without detracting from the musical score. In order to facilitate audience comprehension, he had a speaker, dressed in evening clothes, introduce and explain each of the six episodes in French.

Theodore Stravinsky, the composer's eldest son, designed a special set that was to have been built on a higher platform, to project the singers' voices right into the auditorium. The chorus was to stand on three levels with only their heads appearing over a drapery in bas-relief style. The protagonists would look like living statues in costumes and masks conceived by Cocteau. The masks consisted of eyes fastened to bits of wood, hair made of raffia, with ears, noses, and mouths constructed with pieces of wire and cork.[23] The actors' gestures were to be stylized; only their arms and heads would move.

Because of the limited funds at their disposal, the first performance of *Oedipus Rex* at the Theatre Sarah Bernhardt on 30 May 1927 with Stravinsky conducting had to be performed as an oratorio without masks or costumes. It was preceded and followed by ballets performed by Diaghilev's company. The audience was surprised at the great difference between the three offerings and was seemingly unable "to concentrate on something purely auditory." But in 1928 *Oedipus Rex* was performed in Berlin under the baton of Otto Klemperer, featuring sets and costumes by Wald Dulberg. Its full impact at that time was appreciated and yet, despite this success, *Oedipus Rex* has never become a popular work.[24]

## *Opium*

They are intended for smokers, for the sick, for unknown friends, recruited through books and who are the sole excuse for writing.[25]

Cocteau had once again begun smoking opium. He wondered whether this was not due to the fact that he had been incompletely cured of his addiction the first time. In December 1928 he once again entered a clinic, this time at Saint-Cloud near Paris, and he remained there until April 1929. During those weeks of anguish, pain, and panic he felt the need to try to understand his addiction, to describe once again the visions he had while drugged. The work that emerged from this experience was called simply, *Opium*.

In fact, Cocteau noted in *Opium*, that most of his works, after and including *Potomak*, were written in a state of semiconsciousness. In this hazy and dazed condition, free association as well as the narration of dreams allowed his subliminal realm to convey fresh images and new sensations, opening him up directly to the deepest layers of his being. Such forays into his inner world as Cocteau undertook, became in time implicit in his literary technique.

*Opium* is to an extent a diary that Cocteau kept as he was being cured of his addiction. It consists of a series of notes and drawings and is addressed to smokers of opium, to the sick, and to friends. *Opium* traces the several stages in the withdrawal from the Circe-like world of fantasy. To experience such a drama, Cocteau wrote, is like seeing a motion picture in color at high speed; the visions are sinister, beautiful, frenetic, and frightening. The drawings Cocteau included in this volume are a mixture of abstractions and caricatures, full of symbolism of the most esoteric and sensual sort.

Cocteau was pronounced cured and left the clinic. He resumed his active life in Paris, when another event occurred which had far-reaching consequences for his life. Cocteau had met Jean Desbordes, the author of the scandalous work *I Adore* (*J'adore*). He agreed to write a preface for this work, thus lending his respected name to a book that depicted a variety of sexual fantasies in the most concrete and specific of ways.

Maritain was shocked by Cocteau's action. Claudel and Jammes sent him ferocious letters, convinced that he had been exorcised by the devil. Cocteau, annoyed by what he considered to be Maritain's petty and biased attitude, not to speak of the more pointed views of the other members of his conservative group, declared that he had wished to liberate himself from the influence these men had had upon him and used the preface to *I Adore* as an "excuse" for doing so:

I do not hesitate to preface or to push *I Adore* with all my power even if I am to be victimized for doing so; despite whatever a Catholic mind might consider at first glance to be troublesome; because I judge only from the heart. I would not be able to follow a course, without losing my footing, which forces theologians to prefer organized disbelief to unpolished faith.[26]

Now Cocteau felt himself to be really free—to roam around the literary and spiritual world unhampered and untaxed by the constricting influences of his dogmatic friends.

# Chapter Five
# The Struggle
## 1930–36

True realism consists in revealing the surprising things which
habit keeps covered and prevents us from seeing.[1]

## The Human Voice

The author . . . gave this act to the Comédie-Française in order to do away
with one of the worst prejudices: the grudge the young theatre bears against
the official stage.[2]

When the Comédie-Française accepted Cocteau's play *The Human Voice*,
it seemed as though fate had taken a kindly turn. To be performed by
this august group, however, meant in fact a return to the fold, to
tradition. The news, therefore, of Cocteau's latest theatrical venture,
set literary Paris aflame. Some writers cried treason; others approved
Cocteau's move.

It must be recalled that Cocteau had a very special feeling toward the
Comédie-Française. He remembered with joy the exciting years of his
childhood and youth, when he used to go to this theater frequently to
see the "*monstres sacrés*" perform: de Max, Mounet-Sully, Sarah Bernhardt. And after all, was it not de Max who had given Cocteau his
entrée into public life?

Exhilaration marked the poet's features even before *The Human Voice*,
a one-character play, opened on 17 February 1930. He remarked:

Perhaps the idea of having only one character on the stage came from my
childhood. I used to see my mother, wearing a d collet dress, leave for the
Comédie-Française. Mounet-Sully performed *La Grève des Forgerons* and
*L'Enigme* by Hervieu. He acted this monologue surrounded by extras consist-
ing of the Sociétaires dressed as judges, members of the jury, and policemen.
I used to dream about this theatre and I did not suspect that, with its gilt
and its spectacle, it was so close to Guignolo. I wondered how a single actor
could act a play.[3]

*The Human Voice* is in certain respects a Boulevard piece, possessing the usual suspense and plot.[4] Its distinction derives from Cocteau's trademarks: simplicity, straightforwardness, and poetic language. Also, it places the female character in an unfortunate light: indeed, she is victimized on every score. The punitive weapon in this work is the telephone, the deus ex machina, "the banal accessory to modern plays."

*The Human Voice* opens on a room decorated by Christian Bérard. It is heavily draped. Berthe Bovy, the actress for whom Cocteau had written the play, is on stage. Audiences see her as she talks to her lover on the telephone. He has decided to break up their romance and marry someone else. The rejected mistress, in an extraordinarily exciting and demanding role, scales the full range of feminine emotions; never, however, bitter or ironic. Cocteau warns that she must not try to ensnare the man or give him the impression that she is "bleeding" or "losing all of her blood, like a lame animal." She must bear her pain, heroically—until the end.

*The Human Voice* was very well received, and much of the criticism leveled against Cocteau subsided in time. But no work as yet written by this author earned the universal acclaim of his next novel *Children of the Game* (*Les Enfants terribles*). A success at the time of publication, its fame and popularity have increased with the years.

## Children of the Game

Whatever the cost, the most important thing was to return to this reality of childhood: a grave, heroic, mysterious reality, implemented by humble details and the magic of which is most brutally disturbed by the queries of adults.[5]

*The Children of the Game* was conceived at the Saint-Cloud Clinic when Cocteau was trying to rid himself of his drug addiction. It was written after his release, in record-breaking time, in three weeks at the rate of seventeen pages a day. It is Cocteau's great work: a novel possessing the force, the tension, poetry, and religious flavor of an authentic Greek tragedy. The characters in this novel, however, are quite different from their ancient forebears. Cocteau's protagonists, unlike their ancestors, are endowed with modern marionettelike qualities, and they react to the strings jiggled by destiny in a brittle, seemingly unfeeling manner.

From the very outset of the novel, Cocteau plunges his readers into a double world, at once actual and mythical. The work, therefore, has a metaphysical quality with a strong sense of the ominous and the occult. Juxtaposed to this other-worldly atmosphere, over which no one seems to have any control, is the everyday functional world in which the protagonists live. The intertwining of both of these worlds creates a work unique in French literature.

*The Children of the Game,* somewhat autobiographical, opens in a simple, orderly fashion with a statement identifying the location of the action: the snow-covered Monthiers, a street in Paris opposite the Lycée Condorcet schoolyard where the students play during their recreation periods. Since Cocteau had gone to the Lycée Condorcet, the descriptions of the area and the children at play are precise and lifelike. Just as the reader feels himself to be on solid ground, a strange incident occurs. Dargelos, the school bully, throws a snowball at Paul, a rather frail boy whose admiration for him knows no bounds. The snowball hits Paul in the chest, and he falls to the ground bleeding. Why should a simple snowball cause Paul such a deep and serious wound?

The school authorities, apprised of the accident, accuse Dargelos of having inserted a rock into the snowball, and he is expelled from the school. Meanwhile, Gerárd, Paul's friend, takes him home. Paul's home is extraordinary. It is devoid of nearly all adult supervision. There is no father. The mother is an invalid who will die shortly. There is a fleeting glimpse of a maid. Elisabeth, Paul's sister, takes over. She puts her brother to bed where he remains for several months convalescing. She cares for him as does a mother, yet with a kind of twisted detachment and coldness.

Elisabeth becomes the dominant figure now. Her brother and Gérard revolve around her. The three turn the room they now share into a private sanctuary, a place of mystery and magic that only children can comprehend and enjoy. Objects (such as a pin, a box, old programs, torn newspaper clippings, etc.) are transformed by the children's imagination into veritable fetishes; rituals are enacted; certain dates commemorated. Agathe, Elisabeth's friend, is admitted at a later date into this room of make believe and moves into the house as had Gérard. The children pursue their fantasies and frequently do not emerge from their house for weeks on end. Instincts and emotions become manifest now: love, hate, incest. Elisabeth, we learn, nourishes an all-consuming, yet unavowed, passion for her brother Paul and is jealous of anyone or anything that approaches him or even attracts his attention.

Though there is no notion of time per se in this novel, the reader learns that years pass. Elisabeth meets Michael. He is pleasant, unassuming—and rich. She marries him so that she can continue to support her brother and friends. Michael is killed in an automobile accident before the marriage can be consummated. Meanwhile, undetected by Elisabeth, Agathe and Paul fall in love. When Elisabeth first becomes aware of this turn of events, she is beside herself with jealousy and immediately seeks to destroy the love. She thinks up an "ideal" plan. She tells Agathe that Gérard loves her and informs Gérard that Agathe feels similarly about him. Gérard, in fact, adores Elisabeth but does not dare reveal his feelings for fear of being rejected. Elisabeth has now become a matriarchal figure: strong, powerful, and domineering. She radiates over all the other protagonists in this work.

Agathe and Gérard marry according to Elisabeth's plan, thinking that each will make the other one happy. Instead, they are torn with pain. The mysterious and ominous Dargelos appears again. Gérard meets him by chance in the street. Dargelos gives him some poison in the form of a black ball, for Paul. Desperate because of his unrequited love for Agathe, Paul sees no further use in living, and takes the poison. Elisabeth, tortured by the loss of her brother, shoots herself. As she falls, she hits the screen, which had kept the children's room partially hidden; it now topples over; thereby putting an end to the secret world of play and fantasy.

*The Children of the Game* is an allegory that expresses, through its symbolism, the tragedy of human destiny. As in Greek drama, an outside event or force is needed to set the dramatic mechanism in motion, so in Cocteau's novel, the white snowball which Dargelos hurls at Paul acts as the catalyst. This act symbolizes destiny, irrevocable and all-powerful. The throwing of the snowball also represents an intrusion from the outside into the inner world of the innocent dreamers. At the end of the novel, a similar event occurs: Fate (Dargelos) sends the poison to Paul.

Fate's role in the story, the symbolism of the events reported, and the enigmatic and "mysterious" nature of the protagonists, combine to give *The Children of the Game* a religious quality. Like a liturgical drama it has its gods and goddesses, its hierarchy, ritual, incantations—all played out by five children: Dargelos, Elisabeth, Paul, Agathe, and Gérard.[6]

Dargelos is the supreme god in this hierarchy, the master of the children's universe. He is Jupiter who casts his thunderbolts whenever he seeks to mold events. He can be worshiped as a god because he is removed from the four protagonists and, therefore, remains an elusive and mysterious figure. No tangible information is given about him, and consequently he achieves a supernatural glow in the children's imagination. Yet, in *Professional Secrets,* Cocteau writes the following about Dargelos: "He was handsome, let me add: he had the beauty of an animal, of a tree, of a stream, that insolent beauty which is only heightened by filth, which seems unaware of itself, which turns to advantage its every resource and needs merely to appear in order to persuade."[7] Furthermore, Dargelos is the deus ex machina of the drama, a dispenser of poison and evil. He is the leader of events, the creator of the children's play world, since he brought them together, as well as its destroyer.

For Cocteau, Dargelos symbolizes the "dazzling dunce," the forceful, handsome, and artful adolescent who knows how to dominate a group of youngsters and who is worshiped by them:

. . . the first symbol of those savage forces which inhabit us, that the social machine tries to kill in us; and which manoeuvers individuals, over and beyond good and evil. . . .[8]

Elisabeth is Dargelos's female counterpart. She takes over the reins when he vanishes from view. Elisabeth is a vestal in her "white dress," a "pythoness, a sacred virgin."[9] She is like the Sphinx (*The Infernal Machine*), insolent, selfish, manipulating the strands of destiny to suit her own purposes: "Nocturnal spider, she pursues her course, dragging her thread, sewing . . . on all sides of the night, heavy, indefatigable." She is, for the most part, the leader in the children's games, the inventor of the special language (vocabulary and verb tenses) that makes up their prayers and litanies. Many things to the children around her, the guise she assumes changes with whatever each one believes her to be: a "Saint" who possesses the "magnificence of a young animal," an "allegorical woman,"[10] a confessor to Agathe, a beloved young girl to Gérard, a guardian angel to Paul. Elisabeth adores her brother Paul and is enraged by anything and everything that might take him from her. Restrained and forceful in word and in deed, Elisabeth, who moves about in stilled tones in this novel, is so powerful and awesome a being that she is above and beyond judgment even after she has confessed her destructive act: her refusal to permit Paul to declare his love to Agathe:

The confession added to her stature, draped her, tore off her costumes of ruses. Her curls thrust back from torment, denuded that ferocious little forehead, making that part above the liquid eyes, vast and architectural. Alone, against everyone including the room, she braved Agathe, she braved Gérard, she braved Paul, she braved the entire world.[11]

Paul's death had to take place because the human love he felt for Agathe could not exist in a religion whose figurehead was an all-powerful, all-consuming vestal virgin such as Elizabeth. Like her goddess-ancestors, Astarte and Agave, those who are attracted to her suffer from a "fatal friendship" that leads to destruction. Elisabeth, a possessive figure, requires all those who play the game, who believe in her mystery, to venerate *her* alone. She could not share herself with anyone and, therefore, demands total submission from her entourage. Only an incomplete relationship, such as the one between Gérard and Agathe, which poses no threats, can survive in the Elisabeth religion. Complete union between her brother and herself (which Elisabeth desires) can take place only in the world of the dream or in the transcendental realm beyond the life known to man. But Elisabeth has to die because, though powerful, she was not sufficiently highly placed in the divine hierarchy to leap over the restrictions on incest imposed by both society and her own conscience.

Paul is a frail adolescent whose personality is still undeveloped. He lives for his hero-god Dargelos, whose pictures he keeps with the treasures in his room. But as time passes his sister takes on certain of Dargelos's attributes. She is strong as is Dargelos, carefree, courageous, and a leader. Paul is totally submissive to his sister and is afraid to confess his love to Agathe for fear, perhaps, of being rejected. He is the weak Narcissus or Hyacinth, the flower-hero who never reaches maturity.

Agathe is Dargelos's double, we come to learn. With the passage of time, the physical resemblance (noted by the children themselves) between her and Dargelos becomes striking. For example, when Paul, Elisabeth, and Agathe compare a snapshot of Dargelos dressed as Athalie in a school play with a similar picture of Agathe playing the same role, they are dumbfounded by the physical likeness. Paul's admiration and love for Dargelos is now transferred to Agathe who resembles his former god:

Now, without knowing it, he had just transferred on to Agathe the mass of confused dreams he had had about Dargelos.[12]

Gérard begins by adoring Paul in the same way that Paul adores Dargelos. However, later Gérard's feeling is transferred to Elisabeth. "Gérard could not get along without Elisabeth who little by little was replacing Paul in his heart."[13] Like Paul, however, he is timid and weak and cannot declare himself. He simply plays the submissive role of the castrated fawn.

Michael, Elisabeth's husband for a day, cannot survive according to the rules of this latter-day religious tragedy. The vestal priestess, the queen, the goddess Elisabeth has to remain a virgin in order to keep her power over all who love her. Fate is there to protect her from any possible breach that could occur; "the room's spirit watched." Michael, therefore, had to be destroyed.

The story takes place, for the most part, in a room that can be looked upon as a church or a sanctuary. The four young people who spend much of their time in this room consider it to be a "sacred place"[14] with fabulous décor:

On first glance, there was something surprising about the room. Had there not been any beds, it could have been taken for a storeroom. Boxes, linens, turkish towels scattered the floor. A threadbare carpet. There was a plaster bust in the middle of the mantel piece upon which eyes and a mustache had been inked; pages from magazines, newspapers, programs representing movie stars, boxers, assassins were tacked all over.[15]

The games enacted by the children are played with the solemnity and awe of religious rituals. Like most mysteries, they take place frequently at night. In the hermetically sealed room-sanctuary, reminiscent of the chambers wherein black magic was once practiced in the Middle Ages, are the secret treasures: photographs of Dargelos, stolen objects such as curtain rod hooks, false pearls, a watering can, poison, and the like. These objects, insignificant to the uninitiated, are endowed with divine power by the protagonists. They inspire them with the same awe and fascination as do religious objects in a church for a believer:

The treasures were impossible to describe; the objects had been so diverted from their original use, had been so charged with symbolism, that the profane saw in them nothing but a spectacle of monkey wrenches, tubes of aspirin, aluminum rings and hair curlers.[16]

The games and the rituals permit the children to escape from their world of reality into their dreams and fantasies. Time and space become fluid and relative; the protagonists can be any place at any time. It permits them also to reject the loveless and painful rational world. The room-sanctuary, therefore, is a magical place; it is a beautiful and happy realm in the eyes of the players. Although the word *game* alluded to by the children in Cocteau's novel was far from accurate, he suggested that Paul used the term to describe the semiconscious state of the child's world.

With the death of Paul and Elisabeth comes the end of irrationality, freedom, and the immense joy of childhood. There follows the birth of adolescence, that period in life when consciousness becomes manifest. Gérard and Agathe survive because they have been able to accept their loveless marriage, a life made up of compromise. Elisabeth (the queen, the divine) remains in the domain of the absolute and, therefore, cannot possibly fit into the workaday world. Paul, his sister's victim (the virgin-goddess), is too underdeveloped a being to be able to live on. And so, with Elisabeth's death, comes the termination of childhood as symbolized by the falling screen:

Her fall dragged one of the screens with it; it collapsed under her with a terrible racket, revealing a pale gleam of the snow-covered window panes, opening an intimate wound, that of a bombed out city; turning the secret room into a theatre open to spectators. [17]

One of the outstanding features of *The Children of the Game* is the manner in which Cocteau catches and describes with such accuracy the protagonists' innermost thoughts and sensations; Elisabeth's love for her brother, for example, which grows with undeniable vigor as the novel progresses; Paul's extreme timidity; Dargelos's bravura. The frequent omissions of rational plot sequences, the starkly drawn portraits of the children, the flavor of mystery and excitement that comes with the introduction of the unknown (Dargelos's appearances and disappearances), and the march of fate (Michael's death) lend an enduring haunting quality to the book.

At the time of publication (1929) *The Children of the Game* [18] was looked upon as a manifesto of liberty, the work of an anarchist. It dared delve into the "secret" world of the child with all of its unavowed thoughts; it courageously enacted the fantasies of adolescence and for these reasons, "This book became the breviary of the mythomaniacs and of those who want to live standing up. " Furthermore, it is a work that gave expression to the general feeling of unrest and rebellion that Gide, for example, had so stunningly described in *Lafcadio's Adventures.* The bravado and restlessness in both Gide's and Cocteau's protagonists doomed them, and all of those like them, to an impasse. These characters were negative, depressed, and in the end destructive; they were ultimately unable to cope with what they considered to be the ugliness that surrounded them. Rather than right a wrong, they sought to escape from it either through fantasy, detachment, cruelty, or death. Only later did the Sartrean hero transform the Gide-Cocteau negative adolescent into the positive, engaged, and responsible existentialist of the 1940s.

## The Blood of a Poet

I was totally free when creating *The Blood of a Poet,* because it was a private commission . . . and I knew nothing about the motion picture art. [19]

The theme of the *The Children of the Game* so haunted Cocteau that when it came time to film this novel, he made the most imaginative use of the medium of cinematography and montage to make his imaginings and his obsessions credible. His frequent reenactment of childhood experiences in so many of his writings and films attest to the importance of this crucial time in his life. A period of antagonism between the child's vision of the world and what is looked upon by him as the restrictive and negative comportment of the adult, is experienced as painful and destructive.

Cocteau's deeply emotional reaction to his early years comes into view at the outset of the novel in the incidents and images described: the snow-covered Monthiers, the street situated between the Rue d'Amsterdam and the Rue de Clichy, the Lycée Condorcet, the snow-ball fight, the school dunce who enjoyed torturing the entire class and who was admired by them as a result. He took these very same incidents, magnified them, added others drawn from his earlier works (*Thomas the Imposter, Opéra, Opium, Orpheus*), and produced his first film, *The Blood of a Poet.*

The film, originally called *The Life of a Poet* (*La Vie d'un poète*), features the poet as the protagonist. It is his story that comes to life in tableaux depicting the pitfalls implicit in carving out a poetic career in life. *The Blood of a Poet* is divided into three sections: the poet who proceeds to draw a mouth that takes on life, that is then rubbed onto a statue that suggests to him that he penetrate a mirror; the poet who struggles down a corridor, looks into keyholes, then shoots himself; and the poet who plays cards and again shoots himself.

*The Blood of a Poet* transcribed visually elements in Cocteau's own unconscious. It contained those images that had always been meaningful to him: a smoke stack in the process of being destroyed, mirrors, mobile and talking statures, guardian angels, cards, door knobs, charcoal, an easel, a hermaphrodite, and the like. These objects, startlingly photographed, owing to Cocteau's rich imagination, immersed viewers in a totally new visual experience.

When Cocteau agreed to make *The Blood of a Poet* in 1930, although he knew absolutely nothing about the art of cinematography, he knew that this medium would allow him to indulge his need to make believe and so to participate in a world where statues moved and humans could walk through mirrors and back again. Indeed, there is a sequence in which the statue derides the poet for having so little faith in his own work and talent: "I congratulate you. You wrote that one could go into mirrors and you didn't believe it." So that his fantasy could roam unhampered, Cocteau steadfastly refused to give any interpretation of *The Blood of a Poet*. Only once did he write: "I could tell you that the snowball fight is the Poet's childhood, and that when he plays a game of cards with his Fame, or his Fate, he cheats by taking from his childhoood what he should be taking from himself."[20]

It was the Viscount Charles de Noailles who asked Cocteau to make a film strip of his drawings and show it at his home. For this work he gave him one million francs, the same amount he gave to Luis Bunuel to make *The Golden Age* (*L'Age d'or*). But Cocteau felt that the French film industry was not really equipped to handle cartoon strips at this time, and since he was entirely free to make the kind of picture he wanted, he opted for an art film. He asked a group of amateurs, friends of his, to act out a series of visual poses, resembling drawings; these would be an expression of the poet's inner life and would illustrate the thesis that the poet must sacrifice his very blood in order to create a work of art.

The net result of Cocteau's efforts was a picture of remarkable beauty. Charles Chaplin, who saw the movie in New York, marveled at Cocteau's ingenuity, his finesse, and particularly the artistry with which he incorporated objects and effects into the action. The mobile décor and backdrops, the still figures, silent in their contemplation, and Georges Auric's haunting music combined to create a remarkable unified mood.[21]

Ned Rorem remarked that when Auric composed the score for *The Blood of a Poet*, "he produced what is commonly known as love music for love scenes, game music for game scenes, funeral music for funeral scenes. Cocteau had the bright idea of replacing the love music with the funeral, game music with love, funeral with game. And it worked. . . ."[22]

*The Blood of a Poet*, one of the early avant-garde art films, is comparable in many respects to Artaud's equally fascinating work *The Seashell and the Clergyman*, René Clair's *Entra'cte*, and Louis Bunuel's *The Golden Age*.

The effort Cocteau expended on *The Blood of a Poet* took its toll. He was in a weakened condition when he left for Toulon on vacation in 1931 and shortly thereafter became dangerously ill with typhoid. It took him months to regain his strength, even after the fever had abated. While recuperating, active as always, he wrote his first theatrical masterpiece, *The Infernal Machine* (*La Machine infernale*, 1932).

## The Infernal Machine

Watch now, spectator. Before you is a fully wound machine. Slowly its spring will unwind the entire span of a human life. It is one of the most perfect machines devised by the infernal gods for the mathematical annihilation of mortals.[23]

*The Infernal Machine* is Cocteau's most original and important dramatic work. It is—as is Cocteau's theater in general—vastly different from the popular Parisian productions of the 1930s, though similarities can certainly be pointed up.

Cocteau's plays, for example, have little in common with the sardonic and rigorously constructed pieces of Edouard Bourdet. An author who harbored no illusions concerning man's character and predispositions, he treated subjects that were considered audacious and shocking in his time with implacable lucidity: sexual inversions (*La Prisonnière*, 1926), the hypocrisy and vanity devouring literary groups (*Vient de paraitre*, 1927), the unfortunate results of marriage of convenience (*Le Sexe faible*, 1929). His masterpiece, *Les Temps difficiles* (1934), as violent and as brilliant as any Strindberg or Henry Becque play, dramatizes to what lengths a family will go for the sake of money: it deals with the sacrificial marriage of a beautiful and charming girl to a "rich" but hopelessly paralyzed idiot.

The "romantic" Marcel Achard, so influenced by the Guignol, the circus and the *commedia dell'arte,* also shares little in common with Cocteau. A fairy-tale world is evoked in Achard's theater (*Jean de la Lune,* 1929), in which a certain fresh and youthful quality is forever present. Though Achard enjoys dwelling in a childhood world filled with fantasy, drama, games, and dreams, his creatures are tender, loving, and gentle; Cocteau's are cruel and brutal as we have seen in *Children of the Game.* Furthermore, confidence and kindness usually disarm the few perfidious types that hover about in Achard's theater; in *Domino,* for example, the wife of a rich industrialist begins to love the poor and hard-working fellow whom she had hired to dispel her husband's jealousies. Such sentimentality and gentle banter as are evinced in Achard's works are banished from Cocteau's dramas where hurt and punishment for transgressions committed either unconsciously or in a distant past are almost always the rule.

Giraudoux, influenced by Cocteau in that he also dramatized ancient myths, goes about his task quite differently. Giraudoux infused a grandeur and a purpose into the myth not inherent in Cocteau's dramatizations, when treating such subjects as war, education, childhood, and morality. Moreover, Giraudoux's beings, totally different from Cocteau's, are unwilling to spend their lives either analyzing ("I don't really like knowing the feelings of others," Helen says in *La Guerre de Troie n'aura pas lieu*) or destroying each other. Cocteau, like the surrealists in this respect, is forever interested in disclosing the mysterious and hidden realm of the unconscious world, discovering its motivations and revealing these in all of their brute force. In addition, Giraudoux's characters are beautiful and are devoid of jealousies, of torments, of physical and psychological sicknesses; his world is a place of loveliness, charm, and grace. Cocteau's vision of life is macabre and fundamentally distorted. Differences also reside in the theatrical techniques of these two dramatists: Cocteau resorted to shock, to the most modern theatrical devices, as we have seen, notably, in *The Wedding on the Eiffel Tower* and *Orpheus.* Giraudoux is strictly a classicist in this respect and chooses to touch and move his audiences by appealing to their heart and soul.

Cocteau's dramas bear little resemblance to the *théâtre intimiste* or *théâtre de silence* that flourished during the 1920s and 1930s (Paul Géraldy, Charles Vildrac, Jean-Jacques Bernard). This group sought to analyze the various hidden movements of the soul and heart by means of brief but well-placed words, conversations marked with hesitations, suggestions enunciated in half tones. The protagonists were usually reticent, revealing more through their silences concerning their inner world than had they indulged in lengthy analytical speeches. Cocteau's theater unmasks rather through symbols and actions.

One could say that basically Cocteau was most influenced by the surrealists: their antirealism (plot and décor), their marionettelike protagonists, their interest in the irrational, their drive to rid the theater of all previous conventions whether they be dramatic, social, literary, or psychological. The outstanding dramatist of this type was Roger Vitrac who, along with Antonin Artaud, founded the Theatre Alfred Jarry in 1927. His theater (*Les Mystères de l'amour, Victor ou les Enfantes au pouvior, Le Coup de Trafalgar*), like Cocteau's, was satiric and aggressive, vehement in its resentment of traditional considerations of family, politics, character, and dialogue. His characters were also devoid of the usual feelings, thoughts, and actions imposed upon them during the course of time by society. But Cocteau's dramas go beyond Vitrac's. He has infused his world with a poetic substance of which the author of *Victor* is devoid. Aside from the irony and humor implicit in both their theaters, Cocteau's has an eternal quality not perceptible in Vitrac's rather naïvely constructed, circumscribed period pieces.

The Oedipus legend has always held enormous fascination for Cocteau. First he had adapted Sophocles' *Antigone* (1922), then came a free translation of *Oedipus Rex* (1925), now an original four-act play *The Infernal Machine* (1932) on the same subject.

The first act of *The Infernal Machine* takes place on the ramparts of Thebes. Two soldiers are talking about King Laius' ghost, which appeared to one of them, apparently wanting to warn Jocasta of some imminent danger. Jocasta and the blind Tiresias come on stage and question the soldier. Jocasta, attracted by his beautiful body, touches him. Act 2 takes place at the same time as Act 1, but outside Thebes. Oedipus is meeting the Sphinx and her friend, Anubis. Oedipus does not solve the riddle, but is given the answer by the Sphinx (Nemesis) because she loves him. She reveals her human and very female characteristics when she becomes angry after his speedy departure. Act 4 takes place in the castle on Oedipus and Jocasta's wedding night. The couple's punishment is enacted in Act 4: Oedipus blinds himself with Jocasta's broach for having killed his father and married his mother. Jocasta hangs herself because she was a party to these acts. The last scene of Cocteau's invention features Antigone guiding her father, helped by Jocasta's ghost, who now assumes the gentle qualities one expects from a mother. Such a transformation in her character is now possible since she has been purified from her incest through death.

Cocteau underlined the already intense conflict present in the Oedipus story by permitting the characters to live in a double world (past and present) at the same time. He succeeded in bringing about such a feat by scenic manipulation. "A scene within a scene" was constructed right on the proscenium. The characters, who lived in the contemporary world, performed on a brightly lit, daislike structure placed in the center of the stage; the rest of the area, symbolizing the ancient mythological, inexorable aspect of existence, was clothed in darkness.[24]

To deepen audience identification, Cocteau put into practice his old credo: the theater should not be removed from, or be a substitute for, reality, but should be immersed in it. The modern scene, therefore, is reproduced with force and vigor. The soldiers in *The Infernal Machine* are contemporary figures who speak in present-day slang, jazz music blares forth from night clubs, and talk of revolution and war continues throughout. This realism makes disturbingly actual the plight of the entire family—a whole society—at the mercy of an inescapable fate.

Though the sense of awe present in the dramas of Aeschylus and Sophocles has been erased by Cocteau to a great extent, the supernatural elements still abound. Images and objects such as statues, columns, a scarf, and broaches take on the meaning and stature of human beings. They seem to act and talk on stage and so become vital to the drama itself, while dreams, miracles, ghosts, and a series of coincidences add terror to the already palpable presence of mysterious forces over which man has no control.

For Cocteau, man is fate's toy and is doomed to suffering. Whatever joys he experiences are merely traps set by the gods to make his eventual agony of defeat that much more acute: "For the gods to be royally entertained their victim has to fall from very high."[25] The universe is a giant unmerciful machine bent upon the total annihilation of the human being.

Man has no free will. Whenever he believes himself to be free, it is an illusion. He is always the dupe of some mysterious force. When Oedipus, for example, is given the answer to the riddle by the Sphinx, he believes himself a hero, free to enjoy his triumph. The Sphinx, however, acts for reasons of her own. Tired of obeying the cruel dictates of the gods, she wants to help a mortal triumph over destiny. Her reward will be her deification by a mortal. The Sphinx's sacrifice, however, is merely another trap set by a still higher force intent upon ensnaring both her and the mortal. She converses with the jackal-headed god Anubis, a Cocteau addition to this drama. Watcher of the dead, he is well versed in cosmic matters and points out the inflexibility of fate. "We are not free," he declares. He knows very well that the universe, based on a hierarchy, is regulated by an infernal machine, that one person is dependent upon a higher form who, in turn, is dependent upon a still mightier power, and so forth: "Mystery has its own mysteries, and there are gods above gods. We have ours, they have theirs. That is what's known as infinity."[26]

Every individual in Cocteau's drama is hounded by an ominous sense of fatality. Such feelings are magnified when the protagonists have dreams of the sorrowful nature of what is about to happen. But human beings fail to understand these portents and forge ahead right into the trap. Jocasta, for example, confesses her fear after having dreamt of the baby (Oedipus) she had once had. In her dream this child suddenly turned into a "sticky pulp" she cannot eradicate from her mind. It haunts her continuously. Even after her wedding to Oedipus, when she could be joyous, she senses doom. She compares her room, a symbol of her life, to "a café, a prison."[27]

These objects themselves in this drama augur evil. Jocasta complains about certain objects whose power she senses intuitively, but whose nature she cannot understand rationally: "I am surrounded by things that are against me. They all want my death."[28] Her scarf seems to wish to trip her, to strangle her; her broach is aching to pierce Oedipus's eyes. The cradle that remains in her bedroom even during her wedding night, the very one in which her baby Oedipus had been placed when an infant, acts as a constant reminder of her past. The presence of this object makes the incestuous love scene with her husband—Oedipus— that much more shocking.

The theme of incest is sharpened to the bleeding point by Cocteau's revelation of intimate, and sometimes farcical, details concerning the Jocasta–Oedipus relationship. Physical details are broadcast when Jocasta begins to undress Oedipus, and he, in a dream state, calls her "my darling little mother. . ."Jocasta's verbal confession also plays up the mother–son love; "Is there a sweeter ménage; a sweeter yet more cruel ménage, a prouder ménage, than this couple made up of a son and a young mother?"[29]

The hidden world of the gods becomes visible to man through ghosts and divinations: devices used by Shakespeare, Gautier, and Balzac, among others. With Cocteau these techniques, coupled with his objective and humorous style, aggravate the atmosphere. In act 1, for example, Laius' ghost appears to one of the guards. But the meaning of the ghost's warning escapes them. Man's blindness to such signs and portents becomes in this play, theatrically speaking, almost intolerable. The clear-eyed Anubis sums up the situation when he declares: "Many men are born blind and don't realize it 'till the day truth tears their eyes open."[30] The moment Oedipus tries to discover the truth about his situation, to divine his future, he gazes, strangely enough, into Tiresias' blind eyes. The sage, however, manipulated by the "infernal machine," thrusts pepper into the young king's face to prevent any revelation. Oedipus's premature and momentary sightlessness at this point could be considered a prelude to his total blindness at the end of the play. Though man makes heroic efforts to see, in the philosophical sense, he is prevented from doing so during his earthly existence. Only after death, an initiation into another world, do things assume their proper place, and is a degree of vision vouchsafed. At the end of the play (when Jocasta returns as "mother" and no longer as the "wife," purified through her initiation of death) she begins to *know:* "Things that seem monstrous to men are not important in my world. If you only knew how trivial they are."[31]

The two women featured in this drama, Jocasta and the Sphinx, are endowed with the usual cruel characteristics of Cocteau's other female figures. The Sphinx, though Nemesis in disguise, the divinity of vengeance and punishment, is kindly disposed toward Oedipus. She does not really seek to destroy him, merely to dominate him and force him to worship her. Indeed, she is sensually attracted to this young man, and like a typical Cocteau woman, demands he kneel before her. But when he leaves her without expressing his gratitude and affection, her female claws emerge; she orders Anubis to bite him. As for Jocasta, she is a double figure: mother and wife. Herself a victim of fate, she becomes the vehicle by which Oedipus commits his outrages. As wife she is sensual and egotistical to a certain degree; as mother, she displays qualities of gentleness and understanding.

Cocteau uses a shock technique in *The Infernal Machine* for two reasons: to ensnare audience and to draw attention to certain aspects of the drama that might have gone unnoticed otherwise.

To indicate Jocasta's utter loneliness, she alone is made to speak with a Romanian accent. Audiences were, however, taken aback by her accent. They did not know whether to laugh or to take her seriously. They questioned the author's intentions, even his taste. Many felt that Cocteau had used this technique to circumvent the weakness of the well-known Romanian actress, Elvire Popesco, for whom he had written the part. Such was not the case, however. Cocteau stood fast.

Cocteau levels irony and satire at Jocasta; she is ridiculed. She is seen in one scene making advances to a young soldier who answers her in slang. This act also underlines her sensuality and implies nymphomania. She loses her dignity still further by calling the aged and blind sage, Tiresias, Zizi. Such intimacy destroys any grandeur, pity, or admiration one might have felt for a queen. Cocteau has taken this Greek heroine off her pedestal. She has become a modern, down-to-earth, commonplace woman. Only as a "mother" does she achieve nobility and serenity.

One of the most arresting features of *The Infernal Machine*'s first production on 10 April 1934 under the direction of Louis Jouvet, was Christian Bérard's décor. There was such perfect harmony achieved between poet and painter that the spectacle acquired a balance rare in the theater. Act 3, for example, with its heavy purple drapes, gave the impression of arising directly to the sky; the incestuous bed, standing like an altar, gave the atmosphere religious tones; the red floodlight scorching the stage made almost palpable the trapped family's inability to escape annihilation.

In this admirable work in which the omnipotent and mysterious gods of destiny manipulate man's actions and thoughts, a tragic hero's story was enacted. Like Sisyphus, Oedipus battled against insurmountable odds; he was on trial for having been born, suffering because of his idealism and naïveté, struggling impotently to alter the course of that "infernal machine" which is fate.

It can be said that Cocteau's dialogue was never—until now—so nervous, so direct and filled with such a sense of anguish. Indeed, the critic Robert Kemp called him "a prince of the dialogue."

*The Infernal Machine* is a work that will last not only because of its intrinsic verve and poetry and exciting theatrical qualities, but because it has transformed a profoundly stirring story into modern terms able to move the spectator through laughter (the queen's accent) to tears (the dream of her dead child); through shock (slang) to anguish (Oedipus' search for truth). Furthermore, the introduction of objects used in the platonic sense as living *essences* and harbingers of events, and which are expertly interwoven in the drama, makes the play's impact that much more forceful and terrorizing. Lastly, *The Infernal Machine* is a personal drama, and as such possesses both truth and originality.

## Essay on Indirect Criticism

People demand that poetry be explained to them. They are unaware of the fact that poetry is a closed world where one receives very few people and sometimes no one at all.[32]

For no apparent reason, after the completion of *The Infernal Machine*, Cocteau went through an intense period of anxiety. He felt plagued by some inexplicable evil. This anguish manifested itself, to a certain extent, in his sensitive and thought-provoking *Essay on Indirect Criticism* (*Essai de critique indirecte*, 1932). The first part of this work, *Lay Mystery* (*Le Mystère laïc*, 1928), underlines the spiritual nature of the art; the second, *Fine Arts looked upon as an assassination* (*Les Beaux arts considérés comme un assassinat*), is devoted mostly to Chirico.

•Though Cocteau does not make any new assertions, he reaffirms his belief that the poet must sacrifice himself to his art; must give of himself and his blood if need be.• In fact, after each bit of creative work, the artist has divested himself of some aspect of his being, killing it in a certain sense, since it is no longer part of his living self. It is by means of the experience of creation that the artist gains new insights. In the act of creation new associations arise, preparing the artist for the next creative effort—a kind of rebirth. Sometimes, the artist must live dangerously in order to force himself to bring forth a work of art. ▸

Cocteau also stresses once again his belief in the hermetic nature of art and the necessity of keeping the poet's secrets unrevealed, thereby increasing the mystery and excitement surrounding his work. Solitude is also a vital ingredient to the artist. Just as Picasso retained his "solitude" after the world opened for him, so another great artist, Chirico, did likewise.

Chirico's paintings, on which the *Essay on Indirect Criticism* center, are examined and analyzed through the expert eye of the poet. Chirico's calmness and restraint, his mysticism, and the exactitude of his draftsmanship, all rooted in his dreams, are the qualities that most impressed Cocteau:

Chirico has this in common with the dream that the dream seems to transport us into a vague realm; but really transports us into realms constructed down to the very last detail, in the style of sleep.[33]

The religious qualities permeating each of Chirico's canvases captivated Cocteau. Indeed, they seemed to infuse him with an outer world sensation, grip his very being. Like Cocteau, Chirico's spiritual outlook was devoid of dogma:

Chirico is, in the last analysis, a religious painter. A religious painter without faith. A painter of lay mystery. He must have miracles. His realism prevents him from painting miracles to which he could not add faith. He must, therefore, produce them by removing objects and people from their surroundings.[34]

Giorgio di Chirico, who had won the praise of both Apollinaire and Picasso, was born in Greece (1888) of Italian parents, studied art in Munich, returned to Italy (1909), and went to Paris (1911), where he exhibited in the Salon d'Automne show in 1912. Unlike the brilliantly textured abstractions of the cubist painters of that era (1914), Chirico's works were endowed with a flat, almost dull, surface. The pigment, barely covering the canvas, gave the concrete objects depicted in the paintings a silhouettelike and ghostly appearance. It was as if Death stood against a still background: "Death is the only player which circulated freely and in any direction on Chirico's chess-board."[35]

Chirico's paintings, Cocteau was quick to emphasize, are not abstractions, but ultrarealistic renditions. His reality, however, differs from that of the primitive in that Chirico "shows us reality by removing it from its usual surroundings." Objects (a head, an arm, an arch, a mannequin, a glove, an egg, a fish) are placed in the most unlikely places. For example, in "The Seer," an artificial mannequin is found seated before a painting. The strange and starkly lit environment of "The Melancholy and Mystery of a Street" (1914) imparts an ominous shadow over the area portrayed. The viewer loses all sense of security and experiences foreboding in "The Grand Metaphysician" (1917); things are just not as they should be. A new dynamism arises from the tension created through stillness in "Place d'Italie" (1912): action and immobility seem to be battling it out on an invisible and unconscious level.

Few artists have been able to express underlying chaos with such economy of means, such stillness, as did Chirico. The same can be said of Cocteau's writings. Certainly the poet, at least unconsciously, must have realized the similarity between their visions and styles; otherwise he might not have used Chirico's canvases as a means of expressing his own insights. Both men exercised extreme control over their métiers; both lent a sculpturesque simplicity, a near rigidity of form to their endeavors; both were haunted by a sense of the mysterious, metaphysical power in the universe; both responded to these unseen powers with a counterinstinctual force, making for the extreme violence intrinsic in their work. Both displaced objects, blended modern and ancient themes, placing the most up-to-date mechanical mannequin into historically traditional backgrounds. [36]

A humorous note concerning Cocteau's manuscript *Essay on Indirect Criticism* is that it resembled a Chirico painting. Cocteau wrote it while living in a very small apartment on Rue Vignon. There, he set down his thoughts on scattered bits of paper, boxes, cigarette cases, tennis shoes, tablecloths, on anything and everything that happened to be around as his ideas came. He had promised his manuscript to a lady friend, and forewarned, she arrived with a large sack, filled it with the various objects, and carried the so-called book away on her back, as though she were carting coal.

## The Knights of the Round Table

Inspiration does not necessarily come down from some heaven. To explain it one would have to disturb the human darkness and, without doubt, nothing flattering would emerge. The poet's role is a humble one. He is at his night's orders. [37]

The anxiety that had plagued Cocteau so fiercely during the writing of his *Essay on Indirect Criticism* abated somewhat on completion of the manuscript. He was fully released from it as he finished a new three-act play, *The Knights of the Round Table* (*Les Chevaliers de la table ronde*). This work is a symbolic recounting of the shattering ordeal of his opium cure. Little did his friends realize, when they urged him to give up opium, the destruction that was about to be inflicted upon the poet. He had, thanks to opium, succeeded in maintaining a sort of equilibrium and "quietude," though an artificial one. When the drug was no longer available, his balance vanished, and he had to excavate his own spiritual and emotional roots in order to discover other foundations and so restore some kind of harmony to his body and soul.

The genesis of *The Knights of the Round Table* is intriguing. One night, after weeks of insomnia, Cocteau dozed off and awakened the following morning with the complete plot for a new play in his head. The play that was revealed to Cocteau in a dream, down to the last detail, centered, strangely enough, on a period in history about which Cocteau knew little and had always considered mournful and uninspiring—the Middle Ages. In 1933, while visiting Igor Markevitch in Switzerland, he set down the entire work on paper. The only part of this drama that was invented on a conscious level, Cocteau writes, was the section alluded to as the "talking flower"; the rest had come directly from his unconscious.

The Grail legend, which was incorporated into Christian mythology during the early centuries, was pagan in origin.[38] The Grail theme and its adjunct, the Knights of the Round Table, became a great source of inspiration for writers throughout the ages: the Welsh clerics (sixth century), Chrétien de Troyes's *Perceval,* Wace's elegant verse chronicle *Roman de Brut* (twelfth century), Malory's *Morte d'Arthur* (fifteenth century), Mark Twain's burlesque of the romance *Connecticut Yankee in King Arthur's Court,* to mention but a few.

To the deeply religious, the Grail was considered a talisman. It has been represented during the course of history in various forms: as a chalice, a dish, a cup into which a lance drips blood, and so forth. Christ had allegedly drunk from the Grail at the Last Supper. When Joseph of Arimathaea acquired it, he caught in it some of Christ's blood and carried it to England where it gave him food and spiritual sustenance for the rest of his days. As a result, the Grail was supposed to bring healing and food to those who touched it, but it could only be found by a truly pure soul.

The Grail theme has an inner symbolic significance for Cocteau. It represents a nonmaterial and mysterious force, "that very rare self-equilibrium"; a state that can be achieved only when a realistic attitude toward life, no matter how difficult to maintain, is adopted.

The conflict between reality and illusion is clearly delineated in *The Knights of the Round Table.* To dramatize this dichotomy in attitudes toward life, Cocteau created a series of double personalities: a real and a false queen, a real and a false Gawain, a real and a false Galahad. These dual personalities, portrayed by the same actor, could have led to much confusion on stage, had Cocteau not used an ingenious device to keep clear the distinction between the protagonists. He indicated the use of a natural as opposed to a stylized acting technique. When a character, for example, was himself or herself, he or she acted in a natural manner;

when playing the false aspects of themselves, they assumed different stances, voices, and gestures. Their entire personalities went through physical transformations as well as inner ones.

The plot: the purity and integrity of King Arthur's court have been replaced by a world of illusion under the spell of the evil magician Merlin. Queen Guenivere has asked Merlin to distract the king so that she and Lancelot can pursue their illicit relationship undiscovered. Meanwhile, Blandine, daughter of the king and queen, notices an extraordinary change come over her fiancé Gawain; he has become rude and unloving. She is unaware of the fact that the real Gawain has been imprisoned and displaced by an evil spirit, Ginifer. Merlin is not afraid of anything but Galahad's power. When Galahad arrives at King Arthur's court in quest of the Grail, Merlin sets a trap. Galahad, although seeing through Merlin's machinations, does not reveal his knowledge. Merlin confidently pursues his sinister plans and sets Ginifer, the evil spirit, into the queen. Lancelot, who mistakes her for the real queen, is appalled by her boorishness. A misunderstanding between them is about to arise when Galahad enters and informs Lancelot of the hoax. The real Gawain is then found, and Galahad unmasks Merlin. Truth is restored and illusion disappears. But now—pain begins. King Arthur knows the pangs of jealousy; the queen knows torment and shame. Lancelot and she withdraw from the world of the living into the lake where their pure and ideal love can exist. Though Arthur suffers great loneliness and his life is no longer rose-colored, he prefers this state of affairs. He exclaims: "I would rather have real deaths than a false life."[39] Blandine is happy because her true Gawain has returned and her brother Segramor, a poet who had once been able to understand bird language but had been deprived of his power by Merlin, rediscovers it within himself.

Cocteau sets up a set of mirror images in *The Knights of the Round Table* to dramatize the struggle between reality and illusion, good and evil. These reflections are designed to ensnare the protagonists, to lure them into a kind of false security, a dimly lit, romantic, fallacious existence.

King Arthur, a victim of altered vision, is totally unaware of the false and precarious existence he is leading. He is blind to his wife's adultery and dependent upon the false Gawain whom Merlin has placed in his path to keep his life rosy. In certain respects he resembles Oedipus and Jocasta, whose joy is based on ignorance of reality. The spectators, however, are aware of the true state of affairs (the actors' altered speech, gestures, etc.) and are drawn into the stage action, but, unable to do anything, they are subjected to increasing tension as the plot develops.

The queen's crime is much greater than the king's, since she knows exactly what she is doing, herself asking Merlin to cast the spell that enables her to pursue her adulterous relationship with Lancelot. Guilt, however, is unknown to her because she lives in a world of unreality and romance. Her love, therefore, seems sublime and pure. When Lancelot speaks with the false queen and is taken aback by her monstrous and lascivious nature, this indicates a return of vision and, psychologically speaking, a materialization of unconscious guilt feelings with regard to the queen's erotic and amoral side.

The magic world created by Merlin is evil because it is unreal. He has in effect created a state of paradise, tantamount to nonliving. The queen describes such a state. She declares, "we are living in a dim twilight where there is no difference between night and day, no reason why one should get up or go to bed. Our nerves are all on edge waiting for this inexplicable phenomenon, which is contrary to all our habits, to be over." But Galahad, the light-bringer, the pure in heart, destroys this fantasy life: "This house has been struck by lightning in the sense that the Grail has scattered our circle and interrupted the pleasant existence we were leading." He gives King Arthur and his entourage *sight,* permitting them to see clearly within themselves into a world of reality. Happiness, however, does not always follow vision.

Even Galahad, the personification of purity, of divinity, cannot live on earth as a human being. He can, however, survive as a conception in man's brain, bringing the hope of understanding and the striving for a better life. The Grail, therefore, has been discovered. It exists in the form of a thought or a perception: ". . . it cannot be depicted . . . it shines . . . it is no place . . . it is every place . . . it moves about." It leads toward balance and harmony.

As for the poet Segramore, he can function only in a world of reality no matter how difficult such a prospect might be. Before he dwelt in Merlin's enchanted realm he could understand bird language, but had lost this ability when illusion clouded his vision. The moment the Grail was revealed, he realized that it would *cost* him a lot: "You have to pay, pay, pay. . . ."; he realized that he would experience conflict and pain. But in a state of paradise, where struggle is nonexistent, the poet cannot experience all those elements that spark off creation—life.

It is no wonder that Cocteau called *The Knights of the Round Table* a symbolic realization of his own struggle—opium and a state of paradise versus reality—with all of its pain. He chose vision as King Arthur had, and not the veil: active participation in the experience of life, which includes both pleasure and pain, rather than a state of unnatural repose.

*The Knights of the Round Table,* completed in 1933, was performed at the Théâtre de l'Oeuvre on 14 October 1937. The play was directed by Cocteau, who also created the sets. Cocteau insisted upon extreme realism in both costumes and décor for this production. Even the many stage tricks had to be actual: doors really had to open by themselves, chess men must move across the board unaided, a chair must slip and fall, a table emerge from a wall. All of these mysterious and supernatural occurrences had to be handled in an absolutely matter-of-fact manner, as though nothing unusual were transpiring. No effort could be spared in order to make the fairy tale climate of the production totally credible.

*The Knights of the Round Table* did not receive the acclaim the author hoped for. Because of the unstable political climate in Europe at the time, Parisians might not have been able to relate to a dramatized fairy tale. Certain critics complained that the stage at the Oeuvre was too small to hold the complicated theatrical machinery the play called for; the illusion was not convincing. These reasons, however, seem to be side issues. *The Knights of the Round Table* does not live as a drama because it gives the impression of having been artificially constructed: the characters resemble walking robots and are devoid of true import; the poetry does not seem to flow in unison with Cocteau's life-rhythms. No empathy or sympathy is elicited from the audience. This impression is all the more strange since Cocteau declared this work to have been revealed to him in a dream. Judging from this result, we might conclude that all the images thrust up by man's unconscious are not playworthy. Actually, Cocteau was unable to elicit the warmth necessary to create a convincing play based on the Grail theme. The mystery and magic inherent in this legend needed the tenderness and grace of a Giraudoux to really put it across.

Turning away from the theater momentarily, the protean Cocteau accepted *Le Figaro*'s offer to write a weekly column (for the Saturday edition). This series of twenty-six articles was published under the title *Portraits-souvenir* (1934). In these lively and charming reminiscences, Cocteau brought to life his world from 1900 to 1914: his home, his friends, his theatrical sorties, the artists he knew, the poets in his entourage, and his city, Paris, which glowed like a crystal statuette.

...ed. Yvonne is comparable to Cybèle, the mother of the gods,
...ove her son Attis mad by her insane love for him. He castrated
...f under a pine tree. Yvonne almost succeeds in accomplishing
...me stroke. Michel, however, does not come out of this situation
... He is weak, maimed, childlike, undeveloped, immature. He is
...man, though he is—at least in the play—capable of loving a
...n sexually.

...chel can be compared to Attis, Hippolytus, Adonis or to any of
...oung "flower gods," such as Narcissus or Hyacinth. These emotion-
...undeveloped boys with their female characteristics have never
...d through the homosexual stage which, psychologically speaking,
...human being experiences. Their growth, like Michel's, has been
...ed by an overly domineering mother. For example, Michel's reac-
...s to every incident in the play are puerile and effeminate. He bangs
...he floor when hurt, seeks refuge in his room when rejected by
...eleine, moans, sobs. He is forever embracing his mother, confiding
...er, loving her. He even denies the actual mother-son relationship
...ever referring to her as mother, but rather as Sophie. Indeed, he
...ts her more like a cocotte than a mother. When Yvonne asks Michel
...elp her walk down the stairs, she says and rightly so: "Take my
..., my darling, we will walk down like invalids."[4] The word invalid
...this sense can be understood symbolically, as meaning somebody
...o is partially sick, whose outlook is not normal, who needs help.
...e fact that Michel falls in love with Madeleine who is three years
...ler than he is, and this age differential has been clearly underlined,
...es not mean that he is or has become a man, only that his relationship
...th his mother has been transferred.

...The scenes in which Yvonne confesses her love for her son are volup-
...ous and passionate. They clearly indicate that she lives through her
...on and he, through her. She is the tree, and he is the parasite. Michel
...as no roots, no future without his mother. He is, psychologically
...peaking, living in a permanent state of incest. But he does not die as
...id the "flower gods" of antiquity, because he has created a mother
...ubstitute in Madeleine.[5]

...The father, Georges, like the son, is a weak man, as are almost all
...male paternal figures in Cocteau's works, beginning with The Great
...Split. Rejected by his wife, Yvonne, in favor of their son Michel, he
...takes Madeleine as his mistress, only to discover that she no longer
...wants him, also because of Michel. Psychologically speaking, a cas-
...trated male, he acquiesces to his wife's demands that he get rid of

His readers enjoyed Cocteau's contributions because they felt nostalgic
for an irretrievable past.

Cocteau had won his struggle against opium. He had found his
equilibrium, as is demonstrated in The Knights of the Round Table. He
was in good spirits now and ready to set out on a fresh adventure. As a
result of a bet with the newspaper Paris Soir, he, together with a friend,
Marcel Khil, undertook a trip around the world.

But the weeks preceding his voyage were hectic. Cocteau had promised and written two songs to the music-hall singer Marianne Oswald:
"Anna the Maid" ("Anna la bonne") and "The Lady of Monte-Carlo" ("La
Dame de Monte-Carlo"), both of which had all the elegance and
acidulous humor typical of his writings. For Arletty, a ravishing actress
appearing at the ABC music hall, he composed School for Widows (L'Ecole
des veuves), based on Gaius Petronius's The Matron of Ephesus. This sketch
was a hilarious satire about a rich and beautiful wife who is determined to
spend her life mourning an old and ugly husband whom she had never
really loved when alive. She is persuaded, however, to change her mind
by her nanny and a very handsome guard.

After Cocteau had fulfilled all of his commitments he was free to
leave France. He departed on 28 March 1936. He followed the itinerary
of Jules Verne's hero Phileas Fogg (Around the World in Eighty Days).
Cocteau recounted his trip in terse journalistic style and dedicated this
work, entitled My First Voyage (Mon premièr voyage), to André Gide, who
had once accused him of being unable to relax sufficiently to look about
him and enjoy life.

Fascination and excitement greeted Cocteau from the Near East to
the Orient; from New York to San Francisco.

In Paris again, on 17 June 1936, he was ready to take up life where
he had left off.

# Chapter Six
# The Holocaust
## 1937–45

I remained standing on a desert island; a fantom of fantoms, a shadow of shadows, more solitary than a dream figure implanted there by a sudden awakening.[1]

After Cocteau's return from his globe-trotting tour he was even more active than previously. He undertook to help the boxer Panama Al Brown regain his world bantamweight title; he wrote a regular column for the newspaper *Ce Soir* entitled "Carte Blanche," in which he dealt with fashion, theater and music, and literature. He agreed to let a new troupe at the Théâtre Antoine produce his *Oedipus Rex,* with Michel Vitold playing Oedipus and a new actor, Jean Marais, as the one-man chorus. Henceforth, the handsome Jean Marais was going to earn many successes in Cocteau performances, one in particular in which he created a sensation, *Intimate Relations (Les Parents terribles).*

## Intimate Relations

The theatre must be an action and not a good or bad action.[2]

*Intimate Relations* is a real bourgeois drama in the strict sense of the word with tragic, comic, and vaudevillian overtones. Because of the violence, the satire, and the intense climaxes of the play, it is reminiscent of the works of Henri Bataille, Henri Bernstein, and Henri-René Lenormand. But Cocteau's drama, unlike those of his predecessors, is classic in simplicity, virile in nature, and not at all psychologically oriented.

What makes the genesis of *Intimate Relations* of particular interest is the fact that it was written for and about Jean Marais. The actor, then, played his own character. His stage mother whom he resembled, incredibly enough, was performed by the celebrated actress, Yvonne de

Bray. As rehearsals pursued their course, the ac[...] the personality traits of Marais's own mother, bec[...] abusive and even a bit excessive in her eccentric v[...] the disputes, jealousies, the laughter and tears M[...] stage mother, he told Cocteau, resembled the ve[...] experienced in his own home.[3]

The plot is simple. Yvonne, the mother, su[...] consuming passion for her son Michel. When she l[...] in love with Madeline and wants to marry her, she se[...] romance. What Yvonne does not know is that her [...] Madeleine's lover. Since he has not been rejected by[...] son, he also seeks to destroy the romance. He fo[...] confess to the existence of a young (fictitious) lo[...] distraught he can hardly bear it; Yvonne is radiant. T[...] law, aware of all the intricacies of this situation, wis[...] right. She persuades Georges to tell Michel that M[...] lover does not really exist. A reconciliation between[...] Michel takes place. Yvonne, however, unable to bear h[...] of her, commits suicide by taking an overdose of insulin[...]

The play begins, in the manner of a Racine tragedy,[...] Yvonne's attempted suicide. Tensions rise. Questions are[...] the two main themes in this work reveal themselves: first,[...] matriarch, the virile and destructive mother who seeks to [...] in her steel embrace, strangling him with "love"; second, [...] weak, cowardly, psychologically castrated father.

Yvonne, the archetype of the evil mother, has many [...] both modern and ancient literature. In François Ma[...] *Genitrix,* for example, readers can find the perfect example o[...] ing mother who seeks to castrate her son, unconsciously [...] effectively, nonetheless. Genet's works, whenever they feat[...] are replete with this same life-sapping type, in this case, pr[...] Racine's tragedy *Britannicus,* Agrippina virtually drives her so[...] mind with her machinations. Examples of evil mothers are n[...] in antiquity: Lamia, Lilith who destroyed her children, A[...] murdered her son Pentheus in a fit of religious frenzy, Phèdr[...] her stepson Hippolytus done away with, Attis and Cybèle.

In a Cocteau play, the picture is almost the same. The [...] female figure, usually the mother, must suffer some unfortu[...] she must either die or be hurt for having "smothered" her son[...] destructive force who breathes evil and must not be permitted[...]

Madeleine. Only at the end of the play does Georges emerge as a half-masculine type, perhaps in the same way as did his son. Though he does not have the courage to speak out himself, he permits his sister-in-law, the play's good spirit, to make matters right.

It seems that all human bonds of understanding between the protagonists in this drama are nonexistent. When Yvonne dies, no one seems to be really unhappy. On the contrary, they give the impression of being pleased by the departure of this malevolent force. The crushing atmosphere of dread seems lifted.

Though the hypnotic and miasmic mood disperses to some extent when the curtain comes down, one has the feeling that Cocteau's characters are going to pursue the course destiny has marked for them. None of his protagonists are ever free. They are the pawns of fate, of chance, of their own sick selves. Yvonne had declared, "Michel is free. In so far as I can leave a very naïve and very sought-after young man free." The word "free" as pronounced by Yvonne was devoid of meaning; it was far too restrictive a term and served to indicate only once again the crushing mother personality.

In *Intimate Relations,* Cocteau depicted the grim future awaiting the young man enchained to an aggressive mother, with the truth and poignancy of an autobiographical experience. Michel—a half man—could at best only hope to limp along life's course. Perhaps Cocteau also felt maimed in a similar vein: as an artist, he succeeded in expressing his pain with an economy of means and a restraint, which resulted in an intensely powerful and dramatic work.

In the preface to *Intimate Relations,* Cocteau indicates his intention of being "a faithful painter of a drifting society."[6] Yet, he maintains that this play is not a realistic drama because the family he depicts on stage does not exist in life; it is pure fantasy. Though Cocteau may be correct in his assertion, there is no doubt that such a family, symbolically speaking, does exist in society, and has existed since antiquity. Cocteau maintains that audiences should remain totally objective about the stage action. They should not take sides with regard to the questions of good and evil. The theater should not be a moralizing agent; it is beyond good and evil. Cocteau declared an ideal of theatrical objectivity, yet it is difficult to believe that he took it seriously. If he did, he failed to take into account the audience's own emotional climate. Obsessed with the morbid, the incestuous, and the homosexual, he could not fail to elicit either sympathy or repugnance on the part of the viewer toward his vision of life.

*Intimate Relations* had been offered to Louis Jouvet for production, but was declined by him because he felt it would not be successful. It opened at the Ambassadeurs and ran for two hundred performances after which it was judged "scandalous" by the Conseil Municipal. Such an "incestuous" piece should not, they believed, be performed in a city-owned theater. It was moved, therefore, to the Bouffes-Parisiens, where it enjoyed another two hundred performances. Not only was *Intimate Relations* a successful play, but it was turned into a movie ten years later starring Jean Marais, Gabrielle Dorziat, Yvonne de Bray and played throughout the world. In fact, Cocteau considered it his greatest film success.

## The End of the Potomak

The void on stage was driven with spasms.[7]

In April 1943, Cocteau, in need of a rest, left for Picquey in the Arcachon Basin. He went to the same hotel he had stayed in twenty years previously with Raymond Radiguet. There, he wrote *The End of the Potomak* (*La Fin du Potomak*), the second half of *The Potomak*, a prose work he had begun in 1913.

In *The End of the Potomak*, the same type of novel as *The Potomak* with full play given to the irrational, the well-traveled and adulated Cocteau looks back with nostalgia to the fantastic dream world of his childhood and youth. Never sentimental or maudlin, Cocteau describes certain events that have transpired since 1913, either directly, as in a newspaper article or indirectly, as in oracular pronouncements or fables. A mood of apprehension pervades the entire volume, particularly the chapter entitled "Last Visit to the Potomak," in which the narrator, accompanied by a friend, walks through a maze of "livid corridors." However, these black blotches of despair are relieved by brilliantly humorous passages, as in the dialogue between the poet and his friend in the section entitled "The Apartment of Enigmas." The apartment in question is Cocteau's own, on the Place de la Madeleine. There the furniture, the pictures, the busts—in a state of total disarray—live a double life as objects with a particular function, and as points of departure for studied fantasies. They are in effect enigmas.

By enigma I mean an object or a work of art which would be an enigma without looking like one. Every day objects are enigmas, but you wouldn't think they were.[8]

*The Potomak*'s naïve, sincere, off-handed style, that of the poet on the brink of an artistic career, had gone. In *The End of the Potomak,* we find the work of a mature artist who knows all the tricks of the trade, who is inspired, nonetheless, with a feeling of sympathy for the unfortunate and a profound sense of bitterness and disgust with human nature. Events of the author's life since 1914 are recounted in the usual images and aphorisms; a mélange of fairy tales, paradoxes, true stories, riddles, and maxims.

Despite the satire and humor of certain sections of *The End of the Potomak,* the tone of prophecy is similar to H. G. Wells's *Things to Come,* a novel in which the English scientist predicted the destruction of most of the world. Cocteau's description of the Place de la Madeleine in ruins is frightening in its realism—a microcosm of the end of the world. What might have been one of the most constructive and fruitful periods in human history, Cocteau implies, has turned into an era of chaos and mass annihilation; a gruesome expression of how man can hurt and has hurt himself:

The Place de La Madeleine was in ruins. It was reminiscent of the Roman Forum in its atrocious and disorderly aspects of a burglarized house. Around the Place, except for our area which was protected by some magic charm, the houses were cut open, revealing sections, vestiges of shops, banks, death chambers, apartments.[9]

Cocteau's obsession with destruction is nearly as strong as his preoccupation with death. In these pages, death becomes a tangible reality; "Since the day of my birth, my death began its walk. It is walking toward me, without hurrying." To the question of what there remains of all man's endeavors, Cocteau answers, the work of the creative artist:

One thing remains . . . you must leave a name to your works. These works hate you and devour you. They want to live and want to live without you.[10]

The ephemeral aspect of the human species, man's physical existence, vanishes; the product of his mind, however, is eternal. When the artist learns to accept this fact, to sever himself from his creation, as a mother does from her child, so life can be turned into a less painful experience.

Cocteau wrote *The End of the Potomak* in an attempt to understand his existence on earth and to be able to cope with his haunting fear of death. Each time he externalized what bothered him most, he came closer to reaching his goal of self-comprehension and acceptance.

## The Holy Terrors

The audience—even the war-time audience of 1940—must be under the illusion that the play is taking place in the present which is not a present; that is to say, at a special time when the war might very well not take place.[11]

The year was 1939. The war brought casualties and restrictions. The general mood was of depression and pain. In an effort to transcend the depressed atmosphere around him, Cocteau wrote *The Holy Terrors* (*Les Monstres sacrés*), a play set in the theatrical world that had flourished at the turn of the century, during Cocteau's youth.

What I like in the theatre is the mystery, the remoteness of everything, I like all the things that make the theatre solemn and impressive, and that actually separate us from the public. I like the sudden way the house lights go out, the hush, the rising curtain, the great arch of light above the footlights, and the darkness everywhere else.[12]

Specifically, this work is simply a melodramatic Boulevard play in a colorful theatrical setting. Actually, however, its theme is the role of the theater itself in the lives of actors, and their need for everyday reality. If the theater is a means of discovering a new kind of existence, a world full of sensations, dynamism, and essence of self, then the experience is exciting and healthy. If, on the other hand, it blocks out ordinary life, it stunts the growth of the actor as an artist and as a human being, and he can only live then as a parasite unable to grow or to flower. In *The Holy Terrors,* only one of the three main characters lives directly; the other two experience life through their theatrical roles, past and present. Pain and shock are the only forces that can awaken them from their lethargy and force lucidity upon them in the face of blindness.

The plot of this three-act play is uncomplicated: Florent and Esther, the "sacred monsters," actors adulated by adoring audiences, have experienced something unusual in the theatrical profession: they have been happily married for twenty-five years. One evening, however, things change. A young actress, Liane, comes to Esther's dressing room after a performance, throws herself at her feet, compliments her on her great talent, sobs, and finally confesses to being her husband's mistress. Esther is frightfully shocked. Florent arrives on the scene and denies everthing. Finally, Liane admits she invented the entire story to attract attention to herself. Esther and Florent forgive her because *she played her part so well.* In act 2, the audience learns that the young actress has come to live with the famous couple on Esther's invitation, the ostensible reason being that she will be trained by the husband and wife. Actually, Esther has the idea that in this way she can keep an eye on the situation and prevent any infidelities on the part of Florent! As time passes, however, Esther becomes aware of her husband's growing passion for Liane. To permit "bliss to reign," she encourages her husband to be unfaithful to her, and the liaison begins. Charlotte, Esther's friend, accuses her of wanting to dramatize everything by trying to act in an essentially dishonest and superhuman manner, forcing herself to like Liane as a daughter and expecting these feelings to be reciprocated. Though Florent is fully aware that this ménage à trois is untenable, he does not have the strength to break with Liane. The situation becomes still more painful for Esther when Liane, just before she is to perform *La Nuit d'octobre* with Florent, confesses her hatred for Esther. At this juncture, Esther withdraws from the scene heroically, and moves out. In act 3 Liane has been asked to go to Hollywood. She accepts the offer for both herself and Florent. Florent, however, refuses to leave. Only Esther, Liane believes, can convince Florent to start a new career. She sends Esther a note asking her to come urgently. Esther, under the impression that Florent is ill, rushes over. Florent informs his wife of his disenchantment with Liane and of his desire to return to her. Esther, reverting to herself, accepts his love, and the intruder, Liane, is sent off to Hollywood.

Liane, the least complex of the three main protagonists, is a ruthless type who will stop at very little in order to become a famous actress. She is herself always, and lives in the workaday world, unlike Esther and Florent who have always existed *through* their roles. Liane represents the real world, the harsh intruder come to destroy a complacent and essentially unreal existence.

Esther is a combination of kindness, violence, masochism, and selfishness. She shows her impatience and egotism in her attitude vis-à-vis her dresser and sometimes toward her friend Charlotte. When Liane comes to see her, Esther is never herself. She tells the young starlet of her happy domestic life, comparing her calm existence with the outrageous lives of her heroines. "The rest, the dramas, the intrigues, the lies, the malice, that's for the theatre," she exclaims. But soon, the audience realizes that Esther is not living her life, but rather existing through certain characters she has portrayed on stage. After Liane's confession, Esther is so shocked her mask seems to shatter. But only temporarily. She launches into a lyrical tirade, as Phèdre or Bérénice might have done. Never once does she react naturally. Esther, instead of allowing herself to really feel her pain, identifies herself with a part she once created on stage. Unable to assimilate the shocking news, she cannot possibly accept it realistically and, therefore, must experience it through a character's personality.

Play-acting can be so deeply ingrained within the human personality that it smothers the real one. This is Esther's case. She has existed for so many years within the limited world of her art, that, like Oedipus and Jocasta, or King Arthur, she was happy in her ignorance. Furthermore, she had never really been confronted with a *real* situation before, a threat to her emotional well-being. Now, for the first time in her mature life, Esther is forced to make a decision. Her reasoning, owing to a lack of practice, is as unsteady as are the first steps taken by a child. To ask the young and beautiful Liane to come and live with her husband and herself, ostensibly to improve her acting, but in reality to prevent a liaison, seems ludicrous. Totally unconscious of reality, Esther is driven to live up to the image she has created for herself; that of the saintly martyr. She suffers doubly, because of the jealousy she feels for Liane and also because of her inability to rise above petty foibles, envy, and anger. The demands she makes upon herself, are, in effect, *inhuman:*

My one dream is to stay close to you, and not annoy you, not look like a martyr . . . What I want, and keep praying for, is to live in a way that would be condemned by society because society doesn't know what love is. I want no fuss and no show about it . . . And I want to live that life in all of its simplicity—not defiantly . . . just quietly and unobtrusively, going my own sweet way. . . .[13]

When Liane announces her hatred for Esther, she also ridicules Esther's propensity for the sublime, her need to become the ideal person of her dreams. Liane is the only character who speaks the truth in the entire drama. She sees that Esther at this juncture is indistinguishable from her role-playing. Liane speaks out:

You hate me like poison but you've been turning on the love full blast. You thought you'd get at Florent, being all noble and generous, all heroic . . . Well, I'd had enough of your nobility and I'm certainly not going to act noble myself! I've borne it four months, and all the time you've been trying to blow yourself up and me at the same time.[14]

Florent does not live in either the world of reality or of illusion. He does not live at all. He merely exists and at best as a foil, a prey over which the two female figures are at odds. He is unable to act decisively. When he refuses to go to Hollywood, he probably does so out of fear of starting anything new.

Only after Esther's self-imposed exile does she become aware of the differences existing between her real life and her theatrical existence with all of its artifice and glitter. The shock of reality occurs after an *actual* threat had thrust itself into her life. It forces her to open her eyes to the world about her and live in it thoroughly and completely.

Cocteau juxtaposes three different worlds in *The Holy Terrors:* Liane's real, if unattractive world; the artificial existence Florent and Esther have built around themselves; and the audience's attitude vis-à-vis both of these realms. The audience, Esther, and Florent all fall into the trap set by Cocteau. In the beginning they believe Liane to be a sincere, naïve girl who seemingly seeks to assuage her conscience by confessing her guilt. When she admires her lie, however, another facet of her nature emerges. Strangely enough, by speaking the truth she reveals herself as a dissimulating victim. Florent and Esther, wrapped tightly in their world of illusion, inexperienced in the intricacies of real-life manipulations, victims of the parts they have interpreted all their lives, are unable to see into the complexities of the human personality. Esther reacts as a "sublime heroine" to this painful experience and Florent as a "romantic lover"—types both have portrayed on stage many times.

When *The Holy Terrors* moved to the Bouffes-Parisiens, Cocteau added a long sketch to the evening's entertainment, which he had just written for the incomparable Edith Piaf, *Le Bel indifférent*. This monologue enabled Edith Piaf to express the anxiety a woman feels while waiting for her lover, her anger at his late arrival, his silence when faced with her condemnation of his infidelities, and the atrocious pain she knows as she watches him disappear into the night—perhaps never to return. *Le Bel indifférent* was a perfect vehicle for Edith Piaf's tremendous emotional power, and far more interesting in its genre than the full-length *The Holy Terrors*.

Though audience involvement did take place and *The Holy Terrors* was rather successful after its opening on 17 February 1940 at the Théâtre Michel, it must be noted that it was less than a mediocre play. The plot was trite, and the protagonists' peregrinations frequently sounded like the extravagant vicissitudes related in the memoirs of Sarah Bernhardt, Cécile Sorel, or La Belle Otéro. *The Holy Terrors* is not interesting from a psychological, theatrical, or literary point of view. It is a run-of-the-mill play, and one wonders why Cocteau ever expended his energies writing it.

Actually, *The Holy Terrors* was merely a reflection of the paucity of French theatrical efforts during the war years. Preoccupied with questions of daily existence and physical survival, faced with the threat of deportation, with the many Auschwitzes which had been established by Hitler and his cohorts, with famine, with Pétain's fascistic régime, and with disease, the French had little energy to devote to the arts. Furthermore, new questions obsessed them now, philosophical for the most part. People sought answers or at least semblances of such. They wanted to know more about humanity in general; man's function in society; what type of society would prevail during the German occupation and afterward—if there would be an afterward. How should they bring up their children under such trying conditions? What of religion? Had it succeeded in its goals of elevating man? Was it now a fruitful force or a destructive one? These were just some of the issues that confronted the French people during these years.

Cocteau was well aware of these anxieties. They were in the air. But he had not as yet assimilated them sufficiently to be able to re-create them in a work of art. He felt his inability so acutely that he was invaded by a sense of pessimism. The world seemed to have suddenly grown dark for him; not only because of his country's plight, but because he knew only too well that he was facing a new crossroad.

## *The Typewriter* and *Renaud et Armide*

As a whole, audiences for the most part, are like twelve year old children whose interest is difficult to hold and who can be tamed only by laughter and tears.[15]

The situation in Paris in 1940 was untenable. The exodus began. Cocteau left for Perpignan, a city bathed in the sunshine in the South of France. There he gave vent to his pessimism by writing another play *The Typewriter (La Machine à écrire)*.

*The Typewriter* is not a traditional mystery play, but rather a dramatic vehicle whereby Cocteau can once more dramatize his philosophy of life: that a contrived existence can only bring pain; that reality, no matter how difficult it is to face, is the only means whereby life can become meaningful.

Though Cocteau had worked more arduously on *The Typewriter* than he had on any other piece, rewriting certain sections as much as twelve times, it turned out to be an uninteresting work that showed little imagination, still less depth. He himself eventually repudiated it. Yet it did have certain redeeming characteristics, particularly its central idea. Under the guise of a mystery story, Cocteau tried to depict the narrow-mindedness, cruelty, and hypocrisy of people living in a small provincial town in France. The theme had been suggested to him by a scandal that had actually occurred in the town of Tulle, having to do with the consequences of the receipt of a series of anonymous letters.

*The Typewriter*'s theatrical life was turbulent. No sooner had the curtain rung down on the general dress rehearsal, on 29 April 1941, at the Théâtre Hébertot, than Fernand Brinon banned it on the grounds of "immorality." It was not revived until 1958, when the Comédie-Française produced it in a reworked version. Even then, however, it lacked inventiveness and interest, and, therefore had no chance of real success.

Not only was *The Typewriter* banned in occupied Paris, but both Cocteau and Jean Marais, who played the lead in the piece, were attacked in the press. On one occasion Jean Marais, at wits end, had a fist fight with a "collaborator" newspaperman, Alain Laubreaux.

Incidents such as these multiplied during the German occupation. When *Intimate Relations,* for example, was revived at the Gymnase Théâtre, there were storms of protests by indignant theatergoers, which turned into near riots. The play pursued its uneven course until one evening a demonstration organized by the Fascist group Le Parti Populaire Français made it impossible to continue the performance. Tear gas was used and a riot ensued; finally, the police closed the theater. Shortly afterward the Vichy government ordered it reopened, but to no avail. The Germans banned the play—indefinitely.

Cocteau, deeply hurt by the hostility his writings elicited, withdrew into himself. In his small apartment in the Palais-Royal, at 36 Rue Montpensier, he devoted his energy to writing poetry. The strange volume of verse, *Allégories,* resulted. This slim book includes poems of haunting beauty, with lyrical cadences, and stanzas of varying rhythms. But Cocteau achieved neither the depth nor the grandeur of his early works such as *The Cape of Good Hope.*

Once or twice Cocteau emerged from his monklike existence to create the decor, the costumes, and the mise en scène for *Antigone,* transposed into an opera with music by Arthur Honegger; and to write a pastoral play, *Renaud et Armide* with sets by Christian Bérard and music by Georges Auric.

Cocteau was convinced that with *Renaud et Armide,* which opened in April 1943 at the Comédie-Française, he had resurrected an ancient French form, "the verbal opera," which had been popular at the court of Versailles during the reign of Louis XIV. The theme of *Renaud et Armide* is one of Cocteau's favorites: the impossibility of ideal love. In this respect, it is reminiscent of the experience of Lancelot and Guenivere in *The Knights of the Round Table.* Armide, an immortal, has fallen in love with Renaud, a mortal, and is loved by him. Their love is doomed because it exists on two separate planes, the natural and the supernatural. Armide knows that according to the laws of her kingdom she will have to die after having kissed a mortal. She kisses Renaud despite the interdiction. Her sacrifice, however, is virtually meaningless, since Renaud will have forgotten her within the space of a few years. Only a vague feeling will remain of this one great love.

The sets created by Christian Bérard gave form to the mood of melancholia and pessimism in this work. They were inspired by the Apollo baths at Versailles; the costumes derived from the paintings of the two German-Swiss artists, Baldung Grien and Manuel Deutsch.

*Renaud et Armide* was a success. This was perhaps due to the solemnity of the atmosphere and the plastic beauty of the spectacle itself. Yet, *Renaud et Armide* is far from being a great work. It is a twentieth-century transposition of a seventeenth-century genre, and gives the impression of being artificial. What Cocteau had succeeded in arousing within the spectators' hearts and souls with his streamlined versions of *Antigone, Oedipus Rex,* and *The Infernal Machine,* he failed to achieve in *Renaud et Armide.* Perhaps this classical pastoral held no true meaning for him, and because of this no sincere identification could take place between himself and his characters. The theme of impossible love as it comes through in *Renaud et Armide* is neither effective nor titillating. If

Cocteau sought to create something in the class of *The Infernal Machine,* he would have to renew himself, struggle, and strain to bring forth fresh visions and insights.

It would seem, judging from Cocteau's output during this period, that the war years had not been fecund. The series of articles he wrote for *Comoedia,* entitled "Foyer des artistes," in which he discussed the theater and its interpreters, more often resembled a gossip column than a serious critical endeavor. Nor did his almost autobiographical verses *Leone* (1942–45) offer the reader anything novel either spiritually or emotionally.

This free-flowing, rather melodious poem of one hundred and twenty stanzas consists of a series of poetic revelations. The author tells of a female creature, mysterious, inspiring, and awesome who appears to him in his dreams. She is his muse and is endowed with a personality midway between the Sphinx (*The Infernal Machine*) and the angel Heurtebise (*Orpheus*). She is chameleonlike and adapts herself to the period and place she seeks to disclose to the poet who follows her intensely in his dreams, unhampered by time and space. She takes the poet to lands known to him in both his past and present worlds: he sees Antigone, Tristan and Isolde, Renaud and Armide, and other characters he has created. Then Leone projects a series of nightmarish images before the poet. When he gazes at verses written by him and disdained by audiences, his world turns blank: "The monstrous dream and the formidable awakening." The poet, old and alone now, rejects his muse. He will try to seek inspiration elsewhere. But he feels his strength and power shriveling; his age has brought on spiritual sterility. He lives in perpetual fear: "Must I fear heaven with a thousand million / Looks bent upon bringing about our loss?"

When Alfred de Musset wrote about his Muse one could feel his heart pulsating with emotion and candor. Cocteau's verses, however, fall short of the enthusiasm which results from feelings truly experienced.

Cocteau's sensitive appraisal of El Greco's art (*The El Greco Myth*), however, stands out as the exception to his run of prosaic works. In this essay Cocteau described what he had read into the elongated figures he had seen on the canvases in museums and private collections, likening his own torments to those of the great sixteenth-century Cretan artist. Lines moved, colors blazed, the action inherent in the paintings stimulated a nerve within a Cocteau, who had become so fearful of expressing his anguishes, that they very nearly seemed dead. In summing up El Greco's vision, Cocteau could have been describing his own inner turbulence:

Henceforth, he is a prey to the secret world of the drowned, the hanged, the dead, as seen in their last pose, turned into statues by the magnesium catastrophes. All the faces, all the hands, all the torsos, all the legs which emerge from a feverishly kneaded tube and which they resemble, will stretch, will wind about each other, unwind, throw each other down, rise and suffer the sublime cramps of those who are wasting away on earth. They aspire to join forces once again, with the help of a tempest of banners which will snap in the wind, the pools of light where angels and gods are swimming in inverted positions, in a flurry of skirts and of sonorous waves. [16]

Outside of *The El Greco Myth*, Cocteau's writings seemed to be less than effective. Aware of this turn of events, he was perhaps unconsciously drawn at this period to the film industry where he knew his talents would stand him in good stead. He undertook the making of the movies *The Eternal Return* (*L'Eternel retour*, 1942), based on the Tristan and Isolde legend and *Beauty and the Beast* (*La Belle et la bête*, 1945), drawn from the fairy tale. Each film in its own way suggested the child's world of fantasy and free association for Cocteau. His opening statement in *Beauty and the Beast* attests this point of view.

Children have implicit faith in what we tell them. They believe that the plucking of a rose can bring disaster to a family, that the hands of a half-human beast begin to smoke after he has killed, and that the beast is put to shame when a young girl comes to live in his house. They believe a host of other simple things. I ask you to have the same kind of simple faith, and for the spell to work, let me just say four magic words, the true "Open Sesame" of childhood: "Once upon a time. . . ." [17]

Cocteau's exquisite taste for the pictorial arts, his expert directing techniques, and his intense sensitivity when it came to registering the various moods of the heart earned *Beauty and the Beast* and *The Eternal Return* international acclaim.

Cocteau's assiduous activity, as we know, was aimed in many directions: literary, artistic, musical, and also in the field of justice. Cocteau had always been ready to fight an injustice whenever he saw one perpetrated and to help those in whose abilities he had faith. In this connection, he testified in favor of an unknown, but tremendously talented young writer who had been given a life sentence: Jean Genet. It might be added here, that it was thanks to Cocteau's unstinting efforts that Genet's manuscripts were published.

On the whole, Cocteau felt like a hunted man trying to escape what he knew to be his own present inner sterility; he was searching desperately to extract something new and vital from himself. He needed a catalyst certainly, and he recognized this fact. If such a force were not forthcoming, however, he wondered anxiously how the postwar world would react to his writings—how he would be able to create something that would answer not only his own needs, but also those of a whole new generation.

# Chapter Seven
# A Poet's Solitude
## 1945–63

> One of the last free men is speaking to you; free with all the
> solitude and lack of electors that it entails. I cannot ask for help
> from any group, any school, any church, any party. [1]

It was 1945 and Paris was bleak under a gray sky. The war was over,
and though the enemy had been vanquished, the years of suffering
could not be dispelled, at least not merely by the passage of a liberation
army. The relatively carefree, exciting existence of the prewar Parisian
had given way to suffering, disease, poverty, and instability. Yet,
despite the general cloak of fatigue and pessimism, there was, on the
part of some, a feeling of relief, a desire to build something new from
the rubble, to formulate a positive and constructive attitude toward
life.

Jean-Paul Sartre, the forty-year-old philosopher, had done much to
infuse this new feeling of vitality and activity into what could have
become a society slumped in despondency and negativism. Sartre, the
author of the novel *Nausea* (*La Nausée,* 1938) and the philosophical
treatise *Being and Nothingness* (*L'Etre et le Néant,* 1943), had become the
idol of a group of young French intellectuals. His headquarters was at
the Café des Deux Magots because it was heated, whereas his small
apartment was not. Everyone, he declared, is morally responsible for
his own acts; each individual must carve out his own future with open-
eyed sincerity. Sartre offered the youth of France a fighting spirit,
something to hold on to in a godless and "absurd" world. Simone de
Beauvoir, energetic and determined, seconded Sartre's credo in her
essay *Pyrrhus et Cinéas* (1944). Albert Camus, voiced his approval of
existentialism in his brilliant novel *The Stranger* (*L'Etranger,* 1942).

Paris also boasted of a theater that ranged from the intellectually
stimulating philosophical play to the superficial banter of a Boulevard
comedy. Sartre's *The Flies* (*Les Mouches,* 1943), first produced during

the occupation, drew excited crowds who argued the pros and cons of existentialism, as did his *No Exit* (*Huis-clos,* 1944) and Camus's *Caligula* (1945). Henri de Montherlant, who also explored inner man in such plays as *Malatesta* (1948), was less popular, perhaps because of the shady role he played during the war. Jean Anouilh's *La Sauvage* (1938) and *Antigone* (1942) suggested acceptance of one's absurd situation. Michel de Ghelderode, the Belgian dramatist, concerned with problems of good and evil, was just being recognized, though he had written the bulk of his work between 1918 and 1937. The bizarre characters, hallucinatory visions, and satire and irony in his plays *Escurial* (1928), *Chronicles of Hell* (*Fastes d'eufer,* 1929), and *Pantagleise* (1930), which have something of the fantasy quality of the paintings of Breughel and Bosch, became highly meaningful to modern audiences. Armand Salacrou's *L'Archipel Lenoir* (1948) fascinated spectators because of his attacks on the bourgeois. Andre Roussin's *The Little Hut* (*La Petite Hutte,* 1947), with its light and gay Boulevard themes, attracted rave notices.

Where and how would Cocteau fit into this burgeoning, active, and vigilant society?

## *The Eagle with Two Heads*

My play is written in the form of a fugue. It opens on the theme of the Queen. In the second Act the Stanislas theme takes its place and the two themes resolve by fitting into and struggling against each other in the final chord with the double death.[2]

Though Cocteau had not found the sought-for catalyst, he was, nevertheless, inspired by Jean Marais to write *The Eagle with Two Heads* (*L'Aigle à deux têtes*). He offered this moving and well-structured play to Parisians in November 1946. Full of Hugoesque melodrama and theatrical devices, with passion and energy, this work was colored by the pathos and despair that had seemingly become Cocteau's hallmark.

*The Eagle with Two Heads* was written during the latter part of the German occupation. Tired of the emotional and intellectual constrictions of Paris, Cocteau had gone to Brittany where he had hoped to find solitude and be relatively free from the German invaders. There, he visited with friends who lived in an old castle of the Sarah Bernhardt type, with banging windows, smoking chimneys, and rococo decor;

walking daily to Pont-Aven in the mud and rain where he would gorge himself on fresh oysters. The gloom, mystery, and romance of the old castle plus the dismal climatic conditions of Brittany were the perfect stimuli for the creation of *The Eagle with Two Heads*. The play, furthermore, is a superb reflection of Cocteau's own psychological fears and frustrations at this period, and of his abhorrence of the intolerable political atmosphere under which he was forced to live.[3]

Jean Marais, the handsome young actor, Cocteau's great friend at this period, had "ordered" the poet to write a play[4] for him. He had even specified its dimensions. Marais asked for a drama in which he would remain "silent" in the first act, "cry with joy" in the second, and "fall down the stairs backward" in the third.[5] Intrigued by the challenge, Cocteau's "theatrical" mechanism was set into motion almost immediately.

Though Cocteau's play is rooted in reality, indeed is based on historical fact, its protagonists function only in the domain of the ideal, abstract, and mysterious world of the imagination. The story is modeled on the life of Elisabeth of Austria (1837–98), referred to as the "Empress of Solitude." Her existence was so wretched that she could make it bearable only by traveling from place to place and country to country. She was stabbed on 10 September 1898 in Geneva by an Italian anarchist Luccheni.

The plot of *The Eagle with Two Heads* revolves around a queen (played by Edwige Feuillère) who has lost all interest in life, following her husband's assassination by a political fanatic, shortly after their wedding ceremony. The queen immerses herself in senseless frenetic activity: shooting, hunting, moving about from one castle to another, from one room to another. In one of her castles, on a stormy evening, a twenty-five-year-old poet-revolutionary, Stanislas-Azrael (played by Jean Marais) rushes into her drawing room through an open French window. He is bent upon murdering the queen so as to release her subjects from political restrictions. As he enters the castle, however, to commit his act, he is cut by the window's glass and begins bleeding. The queen, shocked at first, then struck by the young intruder's resemblance to her husband, reacts to Stanislas in her characteristically unconventional way. She cleanses the young man's wound and hides him. Later, they fall in love, as is to be expected. The queen's life now gains renewed vigor. She wants to live, to run her government, and to be the queen she was born to be. Obstacles, however, beset her path. Soon both the queen and Stanislas realize their love is impossible, for political reasons, mainly; and Stanislas, in a spirit of sacrifice, prepares to die by taking poison. The queen, frantic at the thought of being alone again and devoid of any raison d'être, murmurs: "A two-headed eagle . . . And if one head is cut off, the eagle dies."[6] She then proceeds to taunt and provoke Stanislas to such an extent that he stabs her just before he dies. Gasping, the queen cries out, "Thank you for having made me live. Thank you for having made me die. I love you."[7]

*The Eagle with Two Heads*, with all of its melodramatic trappings (a storm, a deaf-mute, shadows hovering about, people listening at doors, pistol shots ringing through the air, banging windows, a double suicide, shock, surprise, a commoner falling in love with a queen as in Hugo's *Ruy Blas*), is also an "extraordinary" love story. It depicts two complex individuals who seek unsuccessfully to circumvent the dictates of fate and live life to the hilt. Their love is unyielding because it is unyielding, total, and absolute as was Guenivere's for Lancelot. As such, it is doomed from the very beginning. Unlike their Gallic predecessors, however, the queen and Stanislas do not accept the dictates of "the infernal machine." They struggle valiantly at first, then "take" death, rather than accept any compromise.

The symbol of the "eagle," which Napoleon used to indicate power and strength, which Stendhal employed when describing Julien Sorel in *The Red and the Black*, has been transformed by Cocteau into a double-headed animal, implying not force, but rather conflict and division. Symbolically speaking, the eagle, as well as birds in general, have come to be looked upon throughout the ages as representatives of the spirit. The protagonists in Cocteau's drama are like birds. They live in a world removed from reality; they exist as solitary and lonely beings in an icy blue sky; they are rarely able to come into contact with the physical (human) world save on those rare occasions when sincere human feelings emerge from a mass of ideal and abstract notions.

The queen, a complex personality, is a woman given to extremes and exaggerations. She is a mythomaniac, imprisoned in her own world of fantasy. Self-exiled from society, masochistic, she is unable to vary her actions or change the course of her pursuits. She gives the impression of being strong and passionate—even violent—as she strides around, issuing order upon order, firing guns, and decrying weakness in others. The queen's personality is dramatized through various theatrical devices: thunder and lightning that excite her, by means of windows that must be kept ajar, thereby implying her eagerness to invite chance. To enhance her sense of power and authority, she clothes herself in mys-

tery, wearing a veil and holding a fan before her face. Her unwillingness to reveal her features implies, psychologically speaking, a desire to
hide her own depths from others, also a fear perhaps of peering into
herself. But this mask and these personality traits that give her, on the
outside at least, some semblance of strength and masculinity, are in fact
barriers to prevent the emergence of the weak, frightened, and helpless
individual she is. Fearful of facing herself, of accepting her "weaknesses," she seeks to smother and extinguish them, pursuing a life of
frenetic and senseless activity. To deepen her disguise, to increase the
distance separating her from her courtiers and from earthly reality, to
complete her inhuman and goddesslike image, she must commit her
heroic or extraordinary act—"an act so savage, strange, and against
nature, that all women will think of it with horror."[8] She commits this
act at the end of the play when she provokes a dying man into killing
her. The Queen is, in many respects, like Genet's so-called hard
criminal—in reality, a weak wreck.

Cocteau, enamored of paradoxes, creates a *dead* queen in *The Eagle
with Two Heads*. "Since the King died, I have been dead," she declares.[9]
To live is to give point to one's acts. Her meeting with Stanislas, whose
resemblance to the king is incredible, strikes a deep chord within her.
At once she realizes that he is her "life" and her "death": life, because
his love gives meaning to her heretofore senseless existence and because
he inspires her decision to reassume her political function and return to
the capital; death, in that he will be the deus ex machina, making her
physical end inevitable. Their pure and absolute love (the only type of
which they are capable) cannot exist in the world of reality. It is
uncompromising and ruthless since it will not permit any outside force
to come between them either in the form of a political idea or of another
human being. (The double suicide for this reason occurs on the eve of
the queen's trip to her capital.) Since both protagonists are unwilling or
unable to accept an "earthly" love, they opt for a perfect and lasting one
through death. And Stanislas confesses: "I realized that nothing was
possible between us, that it was far better to free you and disappear
while at the height of happiness."[10]

Stanislas, the anarchist, idealist, poet, and handsome lover, seeks to
rebel against the existing social order. Though at the beginning he is a
socially oriented individual, *The Eagle with Two Heads* is not a political
play in the Sartrean sense. Stanislas, like the Queen, is self-centered,
afloat in his own inner world, enunciating vague ideational platitudes

every now and then. Perhaps here Cocteau was attempting to increase the play's dramatic import with the introduction of a political theme.

Politics in this play, however, is intimately connected with Stanislas's attempted passage from adolescence to maturity: the theme of growing up. As a youth, he saw the world through rose-colored glasses and could say with vigor: "I came down the mountain where everything was pure, like ice and fire. In your capital, I found poverty, lies, intrigue, hate, the law, and thieving."[11] Maturity entails acceptance of responsibility for life in both its beauty and sordidness. Stanislas tries hard to become a man *engaged* in a cause, in the Sartrean sense. His intention to fulfill his political responsibility, however, vanishes with his burgeoning love for the queen he has come to kill. The whole aborted passage from youth to maturity was managed by Cocteau by means of the political backdrop.

An age differential between the two main protagonists not only introduces a theme in *The Eagle with Two Heads,* but gives this work an autobiographical flavor. Indeed, it is a reflection of the pattern in Cocteau's own personal relationships: Raymond Radiguet, Jean Marais, and others. The theme of the older queen who falls in love with the young man indicates, in this play, a desire to take unto herself the vitality of youth, since her own is gone, and youth's strength of which she is devoid. Stanislas looks upon the queen-mother as something glorious, remote, unattainable, like the huntress-goddess Artemis: "You were shining on your mountains like a candelabra at a ball, and with the cold indifference of the stars."[12] The queen, exuding illusionary power and energy, braving the social codes by falling in love with a commoner, is irresistibly attractive to the naïve, weak youth. His desire for courageous political action in the face of danger is fatally diverted into his unusual and illicit relationship with the unconventional queen.

Neither protagonist is real in the sense that a Sartre or Camus character is—a flesh-and-blood human being who acts and reacts to tortuous experience with heart, soul, and mind. Stanislas admits the "unreality" of their lives when he declares, "When I entered your room, I was an idea, a crazy idea, the idea of a madman. I was an idea confronted with another idea."[13] The confrontation of two unreal people on stage, of two "solitudes," of two abstract notions taking on concrete form, is reminiscent in certain respects of Plato's "Allegory of the Cave." Cocteau's protagonists are like shadows or reflections of one aspect of real people, but never become viable as *whole* beings. They are like metaphysical entities at certain moments.

To dramatize this metaphysical aspect of *The Eagle with Two Heads*, Cocteau injects an exciting scenic play of shadows on stage, rendering the atmosphere eerie and frightening. In act 1, for example, before Stanislas makes his appearance, the lights flicker on and off, a storm is brewing. In such a climate, distances seem to vanish, time moves to an abrupt halt, and life congeals. At another juncture (act 2) Stanislas says, "We are alive in the world, at the utmost limit of all that is insoluble and extreme—where I thought I should be in my element but about which I knew . . . nothing."[14] The general tone of the play grows heavy and awesome. Now, practically nothing is visible on stage but a stove. Only the protagonists' faces, set against a black background, glow in the distance. Something magical seems to have been hurled on to the scene, a spell cast; audiences are ushered into a world of essences, of mystical marvels as the queen beseeches the forces of nature, of God, to permit her love to immerse itself in a supraterrestrial world of mystery, illusion, ideal: "Let our love avoid the staling contact of men's eyes," she declares.[15]

*The Eagle with Two Heads* is replete with strange and haunting rhythms. Indeed, its harsh cadences inflict their jarring rhythmic beats upon the attentive spectators' sensibilities. Rhythmic patterns of speech, in stage business and in the inner structure of the play itself, give it a uniquely dramatic impact. In act 1, for example, when the Queen takes her fan and strikes the furniture with it, her words are taken that much more seriously and made more forceful because they are intimately connected with the aural sense. Cocteau himself described the play as having been written in "the form of a fugue" with interlocking and repeating themes, achieving final unity in and through death.

The visual sense is also provoked in *The Eagle with Two Heads*. Cocteau's prose is ablaze with imagery that stimulates the imaginative powers of the spectator: poetic images such as ice and fire, high seas, waves, tempests, sun, moon, "trees wrestling with sleep and panting with fear." These images are also used to characterize the protagonists: their outer coldness and inner warmth, their solitude and desire for communion, their compulsion toward heroism and their fear of it, their need for life and their immersion in death.

Cocteau's heroes try valiantly to live so-called normal lives. But they are only undeveloped half-beings. The queen is not a complete woman, and Stanislas is not a whole man. They never achieve mutual understanding or acceptance; they experience only extremes of emotions and always desire the impossible. Joy was unattainable by both Stanislas and the queen because they were intrinsically clothed in their solitude, severed from society because of their "peculiarities." To make life bearable, they became mythomaniacs and erected a series of dramatic escapades in which they became the pivotal figures. In this world of fantasy, they could survive, but when actuality, in the form of a return to the queen's capital and the governing of her own country, intruded and with it, bickerings, jealousies, and intrigue, the impossibility of living in the *real* world, of struggling against daily exigencies became too great a burden with which to cope. The queen and Stanislas, therefore, took matters into their own hands.

*The Eagle with Two Heads* was not well received by the press, generally speaking, which considered it too cerebral and contrived. Actually, *The Eagle with Two Heads* has all the characteristics of a well-made play: plot, and suspense. But its melodramatic aspects are frequently so overdone (as for instance Stanislas's grand entrance during a storm); its characters so extreme (the queen's mad passion for activity); its language so hackneyed ("Thank you for having made me live. Thank you for having made me die"), that at certain moments during the play one begins to smile sympathetically. Yet there is something quite touching and moving in this work. It stems, perhaps, from Cocteau's own anguish at this period: his extreme loneliness and his inability to integrate himself into an emerging society. Both the queen and Stanislas had tried, and desperately so, to rid themselves of their solitude (through love and politics), but failed each in turn. So can be said for Cocteau. Though he had many friends and had written voluminously on many subjects, he was incapable of filling the void in his existence.

## *The Difficulty of Being* and *The Crucifixion*

A bit disoriented by the failure of *The Eagle with Two Heads,* Cocteau decided to take time out from his various activities to meditate upon his literary pursuits, to assess the path of his inner trajectory, his feelings and thoughts, and to determine his future course. He felt this could best be accomplished by writing a book of personal reminiscences, in the style of a Montaigne, perhaps, or a Stendhal, Balzac, or even in the objective manner of the Napoleonic Code.

*The Difficulty of Being* (*La Difficulté d'être,* 1946) emerged from this experience. The series of essays which constitute this book are modeled upon Montaigne's and are entitled in a similar manner: "On Friendship," "On the Dream," "On Reading," and so forth. They are as terse, explicit, and incisive as the works of the above-mentioned authors whom Cocteau so admired.

The title *The Difficulty of Being* was borrowed from a statement the eighteenth-century philosopher Fontenelle had made when nearing his one hundredth birthday. After examining him, his doctor asked the philosopher how he was feeling. To this, Fontenelle replied, "Bien. J'éprouve seulement une certaine difficulté d'être" ("Fine. I just feel a little difficulty in being"). The fact that Cocteau chose such a title is an obvious indication of his own sentiments and attitudes toward life at this period.

*The Difficulty of Being* is a kind of summing up, a type of tête-à-tête or sincere conversation the author is having with his readers. The book is devoid of puns and enigmas; there is no attempt whatsoever to dazzle or entice. It is a work marked with earnestness and an intense desire to evaluate his own manifold activities. It includes meditations on abstract subjects such as pain, friendship, and death; philosophical annotations on laughter, youth, mores; esthetic analyses concerning words, style, and the theater; portraits of such friends as Apollinaire, Diaghilev, and Nijinksy; and a series of confessions concerning his past.

In this intensely interesting prose work Cocteau seems to be taking stock of his inner and outer self: his fears for the future, his sense of discontent, his fitful search for ways of reaching the new generation. Cocteau made it known in this volume that he refused to sink back to become part of a dead, a *past generation.* Though fifty-seven years old, Cocteau still felt young enough to re-examine himself in the search for another new beginning.

One of the most outstanding essays in this volume is entitled "On Pain." At this time Cocteau was suffering from a very painful and annoying skin disease and attempted to divert himself from his torment by keeping occupied. He confides to his readers his emotional reactions to his pain. In fact, he is able to describe his physical agony in a remarkably dispassionate way, as though he were in full control of the situation.

In 1946, on his doctor's advice, Cocteau left Paris for the mountains where it was hoped the air would relieve his physical condition and the solitude and change of pace, his emotional turmoil. There, in the stilled quiet of a mountain retreat, Cocteau wrote a poem entitled *The Crucifixion* (1946), in which he analogized the physical and emotional ordeal of Christ.

Pain is personified in *The Crucifixion*. It is looked upon as is destiny, "an infernal machine" which never falters in its calculations, eternally precise and indefatigable in its control of the cosmos and individuals.

> The infernal machine was
> Moved by calculations
> unknown to stage-hands
> in a back-stage of ladders
> forbidden to chimney sweeps
> under penalty of death.

Never in all of Cocteau's poetry has pain been described in such harsh and brittle terms. The alliterations and forceful repetitions give the impression of something pounding away, of driving nails into flesh.

> It was washed torn
> boned sullied ravaged
> punctured disjointed
> raised leaning lying perched
> tied nailed unnailed
> glued quartered
> slashed melted scattered. . . .

Like a symphony composed in cacophonous tones, *The Crucifixion* is a medley of varied meters and stanzas reflecting the gamut of the poet's anguish. His fear of death is close to him now as his own hand. No longer can it be conceived in intellectual or philosophical terms as some distant possibility, as it had been to a certain extent in the 1920s and 1930s. Now, a visible, palpable reality is staring unflinchingly into Cocteau's two sullen eyes. By the end of the poem, the poet achieves a kind of stoic peace. He kneels, alone, wearing a coat of mail, and seals his wound as he begins preparing himself for all eventualities.

Claudel was impressed by *The Crucifixion* and compared it to a Bosch painting. Cocteau could never venture any opinion on this work. He was too closely bound up in the suffering expressed in the poem to be able to speak of it objectively.

Cocteau's present anguish, however, was not comparable to the distress he had known after Raymond Radiguet's passing; nor during those months and days when, as a youth, inspiration seemed to have failed. He was now undergoing a totally new feeling, a very special kind of emotion which intensified as the days passed. It could best be described as a guttural cry from his ultimate depths. It was, he felt, his last chance as an artist; his very life was at stake now, and unless he discovered new inner resources he would be doomed to live in the past, no longer an active force in formulating or even expressing the modalities of the present-day world.

Desperately, he continued his ceaseless activities, hoping perhaps to hit upon something striking in the course of his work. He focused his attention almost exclusively on filmmaking now, which he considered as important an artistic means of expression as a poem or a novel.

## Films, Travels, Minor Works

Cocteau made five films. In *The Eagle with Two Heads* (1947), Cocteau so shortened the text while increasing its melodramatic effects that he detracted from its visual beauty and force. The picture was not successful. *Intimate Relations* (1947), an almost exact replica of the play, was brilliantly done before the camera. The closeups of the facial expressions, the studied gestures, and the slow-paced tempo were highly effective in conveying the emotional antagonisms in the drama. *Children of the Game* (1950) based on Cocteau's novel written in 1929, could not capture the extraordinary quality of the original prose work. Though the restraint, the sculptured effect of the shots were ever-present, the mystery and the cruelty of the children as depicted in the novel had been lost in part. The film *Orpheus* was not a transposition of Cocteau's play, but rather a new movie work in which only certain elements of the previous drama are used. The film was a cinematographic masterpiece. [16]

The movie *Orpheus* takes place in what one would term "no man's land," that area which exists between life and death ("*la zone*"). It features the dead observing the living and vice-versa.

Everything is said in the film. The Zone is made up of the memories of humans and the collapse of their habits. It encroaches on no dogma. It is a no man's land between life and death. The very second of the coma, so to speak, Heurtebise is a young dead man in the service of innumerable civil servants. [17]

Death is again (as it is in the play) personified in the form of an all-powerful woman, but actually she now is merely a servant of Death. Then who is Death? the picture asks. Death itself, we discover, is a mysterious force within nature. Perhaps a dream? When Death dreams about a certain individual, it might mean that his time on earth has ended and he must prepare for his next existence. What of poetry? In the play *Orpheus,* poetry was dictated to the poet by a horse, implying that the poetic impulse resides in the instincts. In the film, a car radio is the vehicle through which verses are enunciated in cryptic terms to the celebrated poet Orpheus; but they are communicated by the young avant-garde poet Cégeste, who is dead. One might infer then that art can thrive from an instrumentality, ancient or modern; from anything in daily life whether it be animal, mineral, or vegetable: a theory enunciated by the Esprit Nouveau, Dadaists, and Surrealists long ago. Cocteau still believed in this axiom, that any animate or inanimate object within creative man's experience can be transformed into a thing of beauty in eternally appealing form.

The use of ultra modern settings with high-speed action and dialogue gave to the ancient myth a combination of actuality and remoteness, reality and mystery, and succeeded in this manner in involving the spectators in the proceedings flashed on the screen. The same can be said of *Orpheus' Testament* (*Le Testament d'Orphée,* 1961) which was filmed at Les Baux of Provence, in front of the ruins of the famous medieval castle which stood high on a chalk-white mountain. This extravaganza included such celebrities as Cocteau (playing the poet), Jean Marais, Yul Brynner, Picasso, Françoise Sagan, and characters from Cocteau's works—Oedipus, the Sphinx, Minerva, Anubis, Tiresias.

Cocteau's international reputation was based for the most part on his films. In New York, for example, he was known primarily for *The Blood of a Poet.* For this reason, perhaps, he was invited to this city in 1949 to co-direct a Broadway production of *The Eagle with Two Heads* starring Tallulah Bankhead, and also to be present at the opening of the film version of this play.

Cocteau, however, was disappointed with the failure of *The Eagle with Two Heads* in New York. But he maintained that there had been reasons for such an outcome: it was badly directed, poorly cut, and the acting was unpardonable. Cocteau, however, accepted this setback as he had so many others during the course of his lifetime. It was beneficial, at least, to a certain degree, he affirmed, as are all conflicts. Conflict, paradoxes, commotion, movement, fire, are all catalyzing agents and, therefore, salutary: "I have often written that the spirit of creation is nothing but the spirit of contradiction in its highest form."[18]

Cocteau's stay in New York on the whole was pleasant. It was not the elegant dinners with the society people that thrilled him most, however, but rather his meetings with the various college and high school students who had come to see him. He enjoyed their enthusiasm and idealism and advised those intent upon pursuing a writing career to be vigilant, sincere, and persevering in their literary endeavors.

After twenty days in New York, Cocteau returned to Paris by plane. On his return trip he wrote a "Letter to Americans" (Lettre aux Americains), in which he set down his impressions of the United States and the difficulties he encountered trying to remain detached from his creative efforts throughout the years. To succeed in the arts, the poet must be an individualist, rely on no one, no political, religious or esthetic group, but only upon himself for inspiration. To remain intact and free requires continual reaffirmation of this doctrine, which is difficult because the freer the poet becomes, the more distressingly lonely he is. Pain notwithstanding, solitude is necessary to creation.

I always speak to those who try desperately to remain free and who must, like me, expect to be slapped from all directions, to the point of asking oneself, when one is complimented, whether an error has not been made.[19]

Less than two months after his return to Paris, on 13 January 1949, Cocteau was en route to the mideastern capitals with a company of twenty-two actors (including Yvonne de Bray, Jean Marais, Gabrielle Dorziat). They traveled to Cairo, Alexandria, Istanbul, and Ankara and toured with *The Infernal Machine, The Holy Terrors, Intimate Relations,* Racine's *Britannicus,* Sartre's *No Exit,* Anouilh's *Léocadia,* and Feydeau's *Léonie Is Too Early.* Cocteau kept a journal of the three-month tour, *Maalesh,* in which he carefully noted the audience reactions to the plays performed, his impression of various people and places, and the great affinity he felt for the past, remarkably alive in these lands.

After returning to France, exhausted but exhilarated by the success and excitement of the tour, Cocteau went to the villa of his good friend, Mme Alec Weisweiller who was to become Cocteau's benefactress from 1950 on. Cocteau's financial condition was shaky. And though he had made several films and was a successful writer, postwar taxes so diminished his income that he was in need of outside help. Such help was

freely forthcoming from Mme Weisweiller. Furthermore, he found
warmth and understanding in her home, a magnificent villa, Santo
Sospir, at Saint-Jean-Cap-Ferrat.

Cocteau was usually at Santo Sospir when not in his own quiet home
at Milly-la-Forêt, which he occupied since 1947. There, he sketched a
great deal and also did many graphic works.

Ever since *The Potomak* (1913), Cocteau had not only illustrated his
own writings, but had drawn for the sheer pleasure of doing so. In
1923 he published *Dessins* which he dedicated to Picasso; in 1929
*Opium,* and other volumes bearing his own illustrations. A strong Cubist preoccupation could be detected in his work in the early days
(1913). It was detailed, triangular in shape frequently, and bore the
marks of distortion. A change was discernible in the late 1920s and
early 1930s, notably in *Opium.* A freedom seemed to permeate his art
work, indicating that Cocteau had finally found his *own* genre, his *own*
way of expressing his feelings. From this personalization emerged figures resembling Greek statues: tall, strong, muscular. They displayed
an outer beauty and vitality which made Cocteau's designs and sketches
appealing to the eye. An ease and swiftness, a power and self-confidence
were injected into his portrayals of flowers, busts, candlesticks, and
various aspects of the face.

Despite Cocteau's excellent draftsmanship, his humor which was
frequently embedded in his various trademarks (the star, for example),
his variety of subject matter, he cannot be considered a great artist. He
did not, certainly, possess the genius of a Picasso or of a Braque, nor
even of a Miro or of an Ernst. His pictorial work lacked the originality,
the depth, that eternal quality intrinsic to the great artist. Cocteau was
a good painter, a fine lithographer, but he was unable to renew himself
from within—to dig up from his own depths the very essence of
creation—an activity of which Picasso was and is a master.

Cocteau's figures, however, amused and distracted the many who
viewed and purchased them. They also indicated to a great extent the
turbulence of Cocteau's feelings at this particular time. In the painting
"The Slaying of Holofernes," he depicted the agonies of the dying
warriors with their spears and shields in poignant terms. Each soldier
wore an expression of profound agony which contrasted sharply with
the implacable grandeur of the moon which shone brilliantly in the far
distance. Reminiscent in certain respects of Picasso's "Guernica," Cocteau also tried to exteriorize man's suffering and did so in a masterful
way, within the framework of his abilities.

A different mood marks the charming and refreshing frescoes Cocteau designed to decorate the City Hall in Menton. Here, sunshine, lightness, and gaiety seem to mark all quarters of the tableau. Though a religious atmosphere enshrouds his drawings for the Chapel of Saint Peter at Villefranche-sur-Mer and the seven stained-glass windows in Metz, an underlying verve and good humor prevail. The delicate and charming sketches he drew for the costumes to be used in a new production of *Pelléas and Mélisande* set the perfect tone for this dreamy and ethereal work. The plates, cups, and saucers Cocteau designed for Limoges are fanciful renditions of faces, bodies, and candlesticks. They make the eater and the imbiber anxious to finish his meal so that he can discover the intricacies of the Cocteau designs which await him.

Cocteau's art work on the whole is decorative and entertaining. The same cannot be said of certain of his minor writings which he was now bringing out: *Queens of France* (*Reines de France*, 1949), a study on *Jean Marais* (1951), a radio series *Entretiens* and *Entretiens autour du cinématographe* (1951), a play *The Impromptu of the Palais-Royal* (*L'Impromptu du Palais-Royal*, 1962), a volume of verse *Spanish Ceremonial of the Phoenix* (*Cérémonial espagnol du phénix*, 1961), and others. These works are vapid and seem to have been written either to please the recipients or to occupy Cocteau. Nothing original or stirring or beautiful abounds in them. The play *Bacchus* (1951), however, is of a different mold.

## Bacchus

One must recognize the fact that certain works enervate, emit unusual and twisting waves, provoke injustice and that the authors of these works can do nothing about it . . .[20]

*Bacchus*, produced by Jean-Louis Barrault at the Théâtre Marigny on 20 December 1951, is one of Cocteau's most exciting plays. It combines profound philosophical insights interwoven around the Bacchus myth, with a dense, elliptical style. The plot seems almost secondary in a drama that deals with original sin, free will, good and evil, purity, the church, and governmental authority. Still, Cocteau did not believe that a play was to be considered a sermon. On the contrary, he felt that the character was the one to express him- or herself and not the author. Cocteau remarked that if he ever tried to impose his way of seeing and thinking into stage conversations or monologues, "the mechanism jams." He added that although a play can have a great deal of dialogue, at the end, his position being clearly incompatible with life (as was that of the Queen and Stanislas in *The Eagle with Two Heads*), which must be lived actively and in a less intransigent manner. Unlike Orpheus, who was stoned to death by the crowd, Hans will be shot by his best friend, Lothar, who cannot bear even the thought that his idol will step down from his pedestal. Almost Cornelian in heroism, Hans is very much aware of his fate and will endure it with courage:

I was very willing to play the role of an idiot to avoid torture, but I refuse to play a role in order to avoid torture, which would make me unworthy of life. The torture would be within me.[27]

Christine is also a typical Cocteau female. Like the Queen in *The Eagle with Two Heads,* in the beginning she is certainly strong, proud, and virile in all of her relationships. Even Lothar, her brother, describes her as being inhuman, capable of almost anything. Hans, however, succeeds in breaking her pride just as Julien Sorel had done with Mathilde de la Mole (*The Red and the Black*). Once made vulnerable, she cries, bites, scratches, spits, and turns out to be very human indeed. In fact, Hans murmurs, "Struggle! Scream! Awaken this sleeping city."[28] But her strength is also manifested in her love, which grows stronger daily. She will leave no stone unturned to protect Hans from the crowds that would destroy him, even if honesty and integrity must be cast overboard. She begs Hans to recant, but fails. Hans, like Galahad, is too strong, too pure, and too unearthly.

Lothar is a relatively weak character. He is, in many respects, Hans's double. One frequently meets a series of doubles in Cocteau's play (*The Knights of the Round Table*). They are usually another aspect of the hero: less heroic, less extreme—one who survives. Lothar's interest in Hans, we readily understand, is really a deep love for his friend, and he suffers jealousy each time Hans dispenses his favors to others. When Hans asks Lothar to be a man and accept the situation (his love for Christine) realistically, Christine retorts,

Don't ask him to be a man. Let him cry like a girl. His cowardliness makes me disgusted with my own. Let us fight and without bothering with him. Hans, you will sign the paper. I demand it.[29]

Hans is the center of a war between Lothar, who adores him and requires that he remain his ideal hero though he die in the process, and

the speeches must move toward some kind of action; they must help the stage happenings gain momentum and move swiftly toward their rightful goal.

The plot is clear. Hans, a peasant whose lucidity has been lost after witnessing the killing of some of his friends by certain lords of the region for the sheer sport of it, regains it after another shocking experience. Wiser now, he refrains from revealing his return to sanity. In this way he feels he can speak and act as he wishes without being chastised. Christine, the daughter of the Duke who governs the region, loves Hans, though she is unaware of her passion, and seeks to have him named Bacchus for the yearly feast. He is chosen and rules the region for one week, according to tradition. After setting prisoners free, entering churches on horseback, pleading for goodness, and relieving the peasants of the tithe, he is acclaimed by the populace as their savior. Cardinal Zampi, envoy extraordinary from the Holy See, a forceful, enigmatic, frightening figure, similar in certain respects to the members of the Congregation as described so brilliantly by Stendhal in *The Red and the Black,* now enters the scene. He has been sent to discover the reasons for the unrest in this region. He is Hans's ally at first, but he quickly makes an about-face when he learns that Hans has done away with the tithe due the church and has, thereby, placed the institution in peril. The dialogue between Hans and the Cardinal, which is the crux of the play, consists of a dramatic and increasingly tense intellectual fencing between instincts, joviality, and goodness versus political and religious totalitarianism. Bacchus, like Christ, believes in "arousing the people," in questioning existing institutions so that a reexamination of certain needs and prerogatives can be made. He refuses to tolerate the status quo that permits Rome to bleed a people in order to pay for a war against the Turks and to build more and more cathedrals. Time is on the Cardinal's side. All of Hans's good deeds turn against him and the crowd—fickle as always—that had once hailed him now assails him. In a fury, they make ready to tear Bacchus limb from limb. The Cardinal offers Hans a way out: he must sign a recantation. While the situation grows more critical, Christine's now conscious love grows more intense. She begs Hans to sign. Lothar, Hans's friend and Christine's brother, is jealous of Hans's affection for his sister. He is also fearful that Hans—his ideal—will succumb to the Cardinal's wishes, and, therefore, no longer be perfect. He lures him out on the balcony, whereupon he shoots him with an arrow. As Hans dies, he mutters, "Free. . . ." But this is merely an illusion. The Cardinal, swollen with pride, greets the crowd and tames its fury by claiming, despite Christine's frantic pleas for the truth, that Hans had recanted. The play concludes on a stifling note as the Cardinal enunciates another *lie* in which there was an element of truth.

. . . Let there be silence once and for all. Bacchus shall be clothed in his costume. The stake shall be transformed into a mortuary chamber and the crowd shall file past his body. I shall say the prayers for the dead and I shall bless this young man. On your knees.[21]

What makes *Bacchus* unique is the manner in which Cocteau fused the ancient Bacchus-Dionysus myth with both Renaissance and modern political and philosophical concepts. The Bacchus myth, so intrinsic a part of Greek, Egyptian, Roman, and Indian ideology, also found its way to Christianity. Bacchus, the god of fertility, luxuriance, and of the vine played an important part, as the Cardinal pointed out, in Roman Catholic Church service. "Bacchus is the God of wine and Our Lord Jesus-Christ changed water into wine. Wine is part of the mass."[22] Christ, like Bacchus-Dionysus (Osiris too), was sacrificed so that the people could be redeemed of their sins, so that regeneration could occur. Christ was resurrected three days after his crucifixion; Bacchus, three years after his death. Celebrations and holy days are reserved for Christ's death and resurrection, on Good Friday and Easter, respectively; so they were for Bacchus every third year, by the Bacchae and the Maenads.

Cocteau affirmed in fact in his *Journal of One Unknown* (*Journal d'un inconnu*) that he had wanted to treat the Bacchus theme ever since he had learned that the ancient grape harvest rite was still practiced (or until very recently) at Vevey, Switzerland. This rite consists of electing a Bacchus every year to rule over the town for one week, at which time his word is law. At the end of the term he is killed, really by ancients, symbolically by the modern Swiss. The reward for his sacrifice is pardon from the gods for the city's sins and the gift of great abundance for the year to come.

Hans, earthly, instinctual, naïve, sincere, tender—possessing all of Bacchus's traits when this god was governed by moderation—refuses to accept the cunning and hypocrisy inherent in the Church and political institutions of his day. Hans, however, is complex, for though he decries the lie in others and refuses the masquerade, he wears a mask, playing the fool to serve his end. Hans is, therefore, a combination of

the idealist and the pragmatist, refusing any concessions to insinc yet willing to use whatever means are at his disposal to ser purpose.

The play's nucleus is to be found in the debate between Hans an Cardinal. Hans bristles when he hears the man of the cloth der thought, considering it dangerous to the Church. "These masque prevent the people from thinking when they relax. A man who t is our enemy. This is the opinion of the Holy See."[23] An intellectu far as the Cardinal is concerned, is a heretic. The conflict betwee two forces, as represented by Hans and the Cardinal, takes a violent turn when the question of free will arises.

Free? What about all the terrifying things the priests hold up to you? walks by dint of trials, punishments, and rewards. Man has made a jud God, because he himself judges and condemns.[24]

Hans is too naïve, the Cardinal declares. The masses must be led spoon fed. Consequently, they have to be given a church with ins tions that can appeal to their level of mentality.

Alas, people believe what they see. In order to spread invisible riches one render these riches visible. People respect only pomp. It must be at the ro our sacerdotal power. It is costly.[25]

A man alone can never succeed, the Cardinal claims. It is only by me of powerful institutions that laws can be imposed and preserved, ma calmed and harnessed.

But Hans is unwilling to pay lip service to any institution or gro He is a loner, as is the poet, willing to suffer solitude, even death necessary, in order to seek truth as he sees it.

If I belonged to a party, I would betray my freedom of soul through t party or this party through my freedom of soul. Besides, my master warned against the moral comfort which flatters laziness. To join a party is to en comfort, because a party protects us and spares us the anguish of choosin between the shades of a color and the color itself.[26]

Hans, the philosopher, is also very much of a Cocteau tragic her Like Orpheus, he seeks to remain true to himself, pure. And purity, " the matter from which a soul is made." He will, therefore, have to d

Christine, who loves him and wants him to survive at all costs. Such a situation is reminiscent, with its strange involutions, of *Children of the Game.*

Expediency wins out in *Bacchus.* The Cardinal placates the people by lying and telling them that Hans has recanted. The established institutions will remain fixed and unaffected. Christine, for the first time, realizes the despicable nature of those who betray honesty in favor of power. Alive now, she is overwhelmed with anger as the full force of reality clutches her.

Cocteau was courageous if not foolhardy in attempting to treat such basic problems as the institution of the church per se: its power to do evil (the Inquisition) and its alliance with reactionary political forces (the feudal barons against the peasants) also, in bringing to the stage the Christ-figure in the form of the drama's supposedly idiotic hero Hans. The play succeeded in offending several important personages, and one in particular—François Mauriac.

As the curtain came down on opening night, François Mauriac, angered by what he felt the play's philosophy implied, took umbrage at statements such as the following which appeared in *Bacchus:* "The people feel that Rome is bleeding us, that we are her milk cow. They have disrespectfully named the Church 'Our Lady of the Collection-Box.' "[30] Mauriac stamped out of the theater on opening night at the precise moment when both author and actor appeared on stage to take their first curtain call. Mauriac did his best to destroy the play in an "Open-Letter" published on 29 December in the *Figaro Littéraire,* in which he accused Cocteau of having attacked the Catholic Church and of having written a sacrilegious work.

Mauriac's attack on Cocteau came as a stinging surprise, all the more painful in view of the intimacy of their former relationship. Cocteau answered in an article, "Je t'accuse" ('I accuse you"), which was published in *France-Soir.* He condemned Mauriac's hypocrisy, his narrow point of view, and his distorted outlook on life. Mauriac, Cocteau continued, literally took pleasure in labeling the works of others salacious and dangerous to the spirit, when, in fact, Mauriac's writings were filled with unbalanced and evil characters who are mired in immorality. Cocteau ended his article with a "Farewell," in which he vowed never to speak to Mauriac again.

Mauriac was alone, however, in his condemnation of *Bacchus* as an anti-Catholic play. Neither the French prelates nor those in Germany, where the play had been performed before Lutheran and Catholic church officials, agreed with him. In Paris, *Bacchus* was acclaimed by first-night audiences in the orchestra, but hissed by the students and artists sitting in the galleries, those very people Cocteau had sought to reach.

In addition to Mauriac's condemnation of *Bacchus,* Cocteau was accused by some individuals of plagiarism. The similarities of subject matter betweeen *Bachhus* and Sartre's *The Devil and the Good Lord (Le Diable et le bon Dieu)* were too great to be considered just chance coincidences. Both plays were composed at the same period; both dealt with sixteenth-century Germany; and both battled out political, religious, and economic questions. Cocteau was charged with trying to ride on Sartre's fame. One fact, however, with which the public was unacquainted, was the friendship which existed between Sartre and Cocteau at this period. Sartre, living at Saint-Tropez, and Cocteau, at Saint-Jean-Cap-Ferrat, both on the Côte d'Azur, consulted one another, meeting at Antibes, on their projects. Sartre had even lent Cocteau, for documentary purposes, certain volumes on Luther and other topics of import which might be of interest to him in his creation of *Bacchus.*

Cocteau had failed to become the spokesman for postwar France. He could not consider himself Sartre's counterpart, nor dramatize the existentialist point of view. It can be said, however, that Sartre's influence upon Cocteau added another dimension to his work. *Bacchus* was perhaps not as well constructed as Sartre's *The Devil and the Good Lord,* but it was, nevertheless, less verbose and far more poetic. In many respects, in fact, it resembled the elegant and austere works of Montherlant, who wrote dramas about the Renaissance era in both Italy and Spain.

## *Journal of One Unknown*

For weeks and even months after the opening of *Bacchus,* Cocteau was to recall Mauriac's smarting indictment of him and the malice with which he had expressed his feelings. Indeed, Cocteau was so hurt by Mauriac's show of ego that he felt compelled to explain the facts related to the incident in his next work, *Journal of One Unknown (Journal d'un inconnu,* 1952).

*Journal of One Unknown,* dedicated to the scientist René Bertrand, is a curious work. Bertrand had become friendly with Cocteau as a result of a statement the poet had made on the radio that impressed him: "Time is a phenomenon of perspective." Cocteau likewise considered the author of *The Universe, This Unity,* an unusual man, who had confirmed scientifically what he had divined poetically during these past years. The most fascinating essay in this volume is called "On Distances." It is mystical in both content and feeling and opens with a discussion of the function and role dreams and peyotl can play in altering man's vision. Such an expansion of vision, which can be achieved by man under certain circumstances, should be used as a weapon to fend off pessimism. Since man can transcend rational notions of time and space, which hamper both his physical and mental activities, he can, thereby, experience to a certain extent at least his eternal aspect. Furthermore, by developing certain elements within the mind, depths are attained, and the unfathomable is discovered. Such perceptions cannot always be translated into a living language, they can frequently only be experienced and remain hermetically sealed within the poet's psyche.

All resides, all rocks in this frontier between the visible and the invisible; what approaches does get smaller, but affects remaining small.[31]

The transcendental experiences Cocteau notes in his essay "On Distances," and elsewhere in *Journal of One Unknown* had also been discovered by Sergei Eisenstein when he was in Mexico. There, Cocteau writes, Eisenstein maintained that time and space had vanished as separate entities. Other strange phenomena had also occurred; indigenous Indian tribes recognized other tribes whom they had never seen before, just from a photograph, indicating thereby the unity and flux of all life whatever its manifestations.

The life and death of man remains the great enigma. It is probable that perspective still exists. That neither life nor death count. That everything devours itself and is transformed into immobility which is an uninterrupted catastrophe, where noise becomes silence; where neither silence nor noise count any more than does life or death.[32]

Other essays on conformity in the arts, false truths, reflections on poetry; and relations with Gide, Mauriac, Stravinsky are also included in this volume. It is, however, Cocteau's profound mystical concepts which strike this reader as unique in his work. No matter how flippant audiences and columnists might have considered certain of Cocteau's

writings, *Journal of One Unknown* remains a document which is marked
with depth of vision.

## Last Essays and Poems

Though Cocteau had fallen short of becoming the new generation's
dramatist, he still remained a popular literary figure. An aura surrounded him now; his works were studied; books and articles were
written about him; and people were thrilled to hear him talk about his
past and the part he had played in the development of the literary and
artistic movements during the early years of the twentieth century. Yet
he was in certain ways a rather "enigmatical" type of person. There were
*certain* questions concerning his relationships with well-known personalities which had remained unanswered. Why had his rapport with
Gide been so distant? Devotees of both Gide and of Cocteau were
intrigued by what seemed a puzzling question. Exactly what had occurred between these two writers to have caused each to dislike the
other over such a long period of time?

Misunderstandings between literary people are certainly not the exception, but rather the rule. Hypersensitivity and a self-centered attitude usually account for this state of affairs. At these moments, authors
choose two alternative paths: they either castigate their foe or keep their
mouths hermetically sealed. Each time Cocteau had been questioned
about his feelings toward Gide, he shied away from explanations. The
several pages in *Journal of One Unknown* devoted to Gide left readers
dissatisfied. They demanded more details from Cocteau. Even after
Gide's death in 1951, when Cocteau was asked to write an article on
Gide, he explained that he could not attempt to explain a man who had
spent his life analyzing himself in all of his works. Cocteau chose rather
to answer questions put to him by Colin-Simard orally, in an interview.

Cocteau discussed the personality differences that had always existed
between Gide and himself; particularly, Gide's paradoxical desire to be
sincere at all costs, and at the same time, to remain an enigma, to
weave a legend about himself. All these aspects of his personality made
it difficult to maintain any kind of continuous relationship with him,
at least on Cocteau's part. Furthermore, Cocteau flinched each time
Gide had condemned one of his works—*Parade, Antigone,* and others.
Yet, despite their animosities, which Cocteau touched upon in his
answers, it must be noted that Gide had spoken highly of *Thomas the
Impostor* and *The Professional Secret.* As for Cocteau, he delighted in

*Lafcadio's Adventures,* perhaps because of the bravura and the objectivity of Gide's style.

Though few and far between, some good memories could be recalled; one such was the time Gide had advised Cocteau to travel and relax. It was after this show of friendship on Gide's part that Cocteau dedicated *My First Voyage* (1936) to the writer. When thinking back upon this incident, a desire to seek contentment through travel seized Cocteau again.

Cocteau had always been a lover of Spain: its poetry, art, sports—and the scorching sun. He now turned toward that country longingly. Spain, Cocteaau wrote, "is a poet." Having been persuaded by his best friend Picasso to take the step and go there, he decided his first stop would be Seville and a revitalizing bullfight. It must be mentioned that Picasso at a certain period had been, and still is, hypnotized by the art of the toreador. He had created innumerable sketches and lithographs with the bull as his subject: lying down, erect, crouching, angered, placid. There was not one facet of the bull's emotions which Picasso had not captured, from the most bestial to the most ethereal.

On 1 May 1954 in Seville, Cocteau witnessed a bullfight. The toreador Gomez dedicated one of the bulls to Cocteau. This was done by throwing his "montera," his black cap, to the poet, who kept it on his lap during the course of the fight. In the small volume describing this incident and his trip to Spain, *The Corrida of May 1st,* Cocteau confesses that the moment he placed the cap on his knee he felt in continuous psychic communication with the toreador in the ring. The *object* (cap) was the transmitting force. It is, Cocteau wrote, comparable in this respect with hashish or opium, in that it is a means whereby time and space can be transcended.

Cocteau's description of the bullfight is precise, and his restraint in verbalizing what he saw increases its tension. It is as if two forceful countercurrents were meeting and smashing against each other: the poet's own overwhelming excitement and his tremendous need to focus and discipline his reactions into powerful, controlled art. One can actually feel the underlying rhythms, the coursing of blood, the uproar, the high speed of the lance as it is thrust into the bull's flesh; the toreador's emotions as he rushes to kill, then backs away with a certain fear as the bull lunges forward. The dramatic effect of this work is quite extraordinary in its ability to seize and stir the reader.

These emotions must have overstimulated the sixty-six-year-old Cocteau because he suffered a severe heart attack shortly afterward. He was bedridden for many weeks. The days dragged, long and dismally. Despite innumerable setbacks, Cocteau managed to regain his strength and geniality.

With his return to life came renewed desires. Now Cocteau wanted to become an Academician. Unbeknown to those closest to him, Cocteau began soliciting votes from the members of the French Academy and before anyone could take him seriously, he was elected a member of the Royal Belgian Academy (1 October) and the French Academy (20 October) 1955.

Cocteau's election to these strictly traditional groups scandalized many of his adherents. To those, the poet replied with tongue in cheek, that all of his life he had always done the unexpected. The honors the poet was to receive were still forthcoming. The following year he was awarded the degree of Doctor ès letters *honoris causa* at Oxford.

In Cocteau's acceptance speech he not only spoke of his past, of the fears he had always experienced when facing "monstrous" crowds, but of the painful and frightening solitude the poet knows throughout his life. In order to create from within himself, he becomes removed from society and ordinary reality and, therefore, suffers terrible loneliness. Yet, he is in desperate need of some rapport with both society and reality. By the same token, special joys are reserved the poet who is hierophant, a priest, a magician, a transformer of secrets, of dark languages torn from the very depths of being. As a creator, he is capable of giving life and form to a poem or a work of art, which must then fight its way unaided into the world of the living.[33]

The artist's role then will be to create an organism drawn from his being, but possessed of a life of its own; whose goal is not to surprise, to please or to displease; but to be sufficiently active to excite secret senses; reacting only to certain signs which represent beauty for some, ugliness and deformity for others. All else is merely picturesque and fantasy-like, two hateful terms in the domain of the artistic creation.[34]

It was, perhaps, poetry itself which had become the most meaningful aspect of Cocteau's literary endeavors at this point. He seemed best able to relate to the poem, to pour out his deepest sufferings in verse form. Pierre Seghers, the publisher-poet, had noted this bent in Cocteau's outlook and suggested he write a type of meditation and, in so doing, try to ferret out his most pressing feelings. *Number 7 (Chiffre 7)* was just such a work.

*Number 7* is a sensitive transcription of the suffering of a poet, one who is a slave to both his Muse and the world about him. Each in turn eats at his very vitals and seeks to destroy him. The former, by overtaking his energies; the latter, through a total lack of understanding of the poet's needs and desires. The "number 7," the gambler's number, which figures in the title, symbolizes the still unborn poem that acts as the author's guide and exists in various forms in all the objects with which he comes into contact during the course of his life.

*Number 7,* more lyrical perhaps than Cocteau's previous verse, is also more tragic; its intense musicality is at times reminiscent of a human cry of distress. The theme of pessimism, the piercing and harsh tones implicit in *Number 7* are less pronounced in Cocteau's ninety-two stanza cryptographic poem *Clear-Obscure (Clair-Obscur,* 1953). After the explosive inner conflict expressed in *Number 7,* the poet seems to have come to grips with his various antagonistic elements, and in *Clair-Obscur* reveals an almost socratic balance. The verses acclaiming such artists and poets as El Greco, Valasquez, Goya, Kafka, Pushkin, the toreador Manolete, and others, are rich with visual images of depth and color; they are light and youthful and impress the reader with their ease and finesse.

The same can be said of *Appogiatures* (1953) which can be looked upon as a series of prose poems. A tone of simplicity marks this work which is also weighted with philosophical import and mystical connotations concerning time, space, noise, and matter. It was as though Cocteau had succeeded in extracting the essence of an idea and had materialized it on paper. The outstanding features in this volume are Cocteau's lucid meditations on loneliness, carved like solitary marble statues on an isolated promontory.

Standing alone. Seated alone. Lying alone. Alone on the grille. Quartered alone by work horses whose croups alone were visible. Hanging alone and his sperm became mandragore. Alone, in speed which doesn't exist, in the minute which isn't.[35]

Though the gnawing, painful, and incessant feeling of solitude is anguishing, it is, Cocteau notes, a necessity for the poet. Because such feelings, "The true, the inevitable solitude of the poet" prove to him that he is still alive and functioning.

This same theme, though expressed in a more visceral manner, marks *The Requiem* (1959–61), a small volume of poems Cocteau had written when recovering from a serious illness. A work bathed in blood, dictated by an inner being that had taken root within his very fibers, *The Requiem* can be looked upon as Cocteau's farewell gift to a world which he had come to love and appreciate. He felt he could now withdraw from his earthly existence with feelings of subdued joy and satisfaction, having achieved his goal—of becoming the poet-hierophant. Now Cocteau was capable of transforming the red liquid—his own blood—into the black ink which spelled *The Requiem* and which had incised itself against the solid white page before him.

# Conclusion

Although Cocteau was versatile and his ingenuity and dexterity boundless, he cannot be considered a true originator in the strict sense of the word, as Victor Hugo or Honoré de Balzac were. Cocteau was a derivative writer; he needed an outside force to set off something within him, to stimulate and generate his own ideas and insights. Apollinaire, for example, implanted in part the flame that led to *Parade* by persuading Cocteau of the utility of abolishing traditional stage conventions (sets, dialogue, and plot), of instituting a new vision that would bring about a total reassessment not only of all of his own values, but those of audiences as well. Picasso imparted to Cocteau a great deal of knowledge about painting in general, and cubism in particular. These insights permitted the poet to create verbal transpositions of cubist paintings. Raymond Radiguet persuaded Cocteau to sound out his own depths, to be in full control of his writing at all times, and never let his unconscious spread forth willy-nilly, as was advocated by the dadaists and later the surrealists. He caused the gestation of such works as *Thomas the Impostor.* Sartre's existential outlook was responsible, to some degree, for *Bacchus.* Once Cocteau had undergone an outer influence (de Max, Diaghilev, Maritain), some amorphous creative element within his personality was triggered; from this moment on he worked individually and alone to bring forth the work of art.

Cocteau's personality could be called mercurial. His energy and vitality were inexhaustible, his output prodigious, and his ability to adapt to, as well as run counter to, the various literary and artistic trends of his day was quite remarkable. Like Mercury, Cocteau was witty and quick to infuse others with a spirit of forcefulness and joy. Though he was a man who adored fanfare, jokes, adulation, farces, riddles, hoaxes, and the limelight in general, he had a periodic need for solitude and retrenchment and a recurring tendency to melancholia. At times the two aspects of the poet's personality (the frenetic and the quiet) worked together, as witnessed by Cocteau's goal of achieving inner balance in *The Knights of the Round Table,* when he came to the resolution that life must be faced courageously. On other occasions there was such conflict between his extroverted drives and his introverted needs that he was paralyzed and resorted to opium.

137

To try to evaluate Cocteau's contribution to the arts, one must divide his works into five principal categories: the theater, the novel, poetry, art criticism, and motion pictures.

In the theater, Cocteau rejected the popular, well-made play characteristic of the naturalistic school, with its flesh-and-blood characters and its real-life props. This is not to say that he fled from realism into the arcane world of fantasy. On the contrary, Cocteau never tried to "arrange" reality nor to "attenuate" it; but rather to introduce a new vision of reality, by accentuating it, as Ionesco was to do in *The Bald Soprano* and *The Chairs* years later. Nothing could be more true-to-life, as Cocteau saw it, than the reality of *Parade, The Do-Nothing Bar,* or *The Wedding on the Eiffel Tower,* where the impossible becomes possible.

Under Picasso's and Apollinaire's influence, Cocteau brought the arts into the theater: dance, music, painting, and poetry. He achieved a unity of the arts in *Parade,* with his symbolic argument, Picasso's decor and costumes, and Erik Satie's music. Later, such alliances of the arts became popular in plays like Molière's *Tartuffe,* with costumes and sets designed by Braque; operas, such as Mozart's *Magic Flute* decorated by Chagall; American musicals with ballets by serious choreographers (Balanchine, Tudor, Robbins, Sokoloff) and music by Bernstein, Weill, and others.

An innovation of the utmost importance occurred with *Parade.* Picasso's sets and costumes no longer figured merely as background but were transformed into formidable protagonists: colorful, if not distorted visions of human beings, assuming an all-important part of the action. The same vital role was accorded to the larger than life-sized, grotesque cardboard heads, masks and costumes created by Raoul Dufy for the pantomime *The Do-Nothing Bar,* the accessories in *The Wedding on the Eiffel Tower,* and the sets in *Orpheus* and *The Infernal Machine.* In much of modern theater, Beckett's *Krapp's Last Tape* and *End Game,* Genet's *The Balcony* and *The Blacks,* Vauthier's *The Character Against Himself,* Fernando Arrabal's *The Automobile Graveyard,* decor is an intrinsic part of the spectacle, as important as characters or plot.

Cocteau, like Jarry, Apollinaire, and Artaud, dehumanized his characters, rendering his theater nonpsychological and as objective as possible. His creatures never existed on a personal level; they were types, functions, symbols, instincts, or inanimate objects. In *Parade,* for example, he created a series of circus types (a Chinaman, a Little Girl, etc.). Each could be anyone and everyone: identityless, characterless, they plunged from one emotional phase to another, never really coming to life as individuals, but remaining formless and amoebalike amid the swirling sands of the collective world. In *The Wedding on the Eiffel Tower,* there was a complete rejection of individualism. Two photographs representing the modern age became the chief protagonists. They deployed all their attributes to crush all personal characteristics. Even the bride and the groom (and the guests), as each uttered platitude upon platitude, came to represent not one wedding couple, but millions.

Since Cocteau's plays were nonpsychological for the most part and possessed of no ordinary plot, and since his characters were not socially oriented, he had to devise a new way of creating audience-actor empathy. He could not hope for the traditional type of projection on the part of the spectators: they could not possibly see themselves in the shadows and evanescent creatures on stage. He, therefore, had to force the spectators into becoming his accomplices. Influenced by Alfred Jarry in this technique, Cocteau tore away almost every bit of theatrical illusion that the spectators might have. He did this by deliberately provoking audiences to laughter at the most unlikely moments, for example, when Orpheus's head remained on stage after his death and identified itself as Jean Cocteau. He also used traps, snares, magic, hoaxes, and shock techniques: in *The Infernal Machine,* Jocasta talks to a common soldier in all-too-intimate terms while jazz blares away in the background. The Queen's vulgarity destroys any shred of empathy audiences might feel for her, and the ragtime music does away with any semblance of historicity in the drama. This premeditated use of unconventional techniques was calculated to startle audiences out of their usual conceptions of illusion and reality. Spectators were induced or forced to give up their habitual orientations—social, psychological, or artistic. They were lured into the author's new theatrical reality and became accomplices in his "game." If they could not "project" or "empathize" with the characters, they could participate in the "game." Genet uses this same technique superbly in *The Blacks* and *The Balcony.*

It should be remembered that Cocteau was perhaps the first to restore and make meaningful again to modern audiences the eternally valid actualities of Greek tragedy. Cocteau's streamlined adaptations of *Antigone, Oedipus Rex,* and *The Infernal Machine* created a new style that Jean Giraudoux, Jean Anouilh, André Gide, among others, were quick to follow with their adaptations of such works as *Electra, Antigone,* and *Oedipus.*

Cocteau was also a master craftsman in the creation of the ever popular Boulevard play with its suspense, its plots, and its general obviousness. His *Intimate Relations* in which he shows the destruction to which an overly possessive mother can reduce her household, is classical in its restraint and its sober poetry, making thereby a powerful impact. *The Holy Terrors* dramatizes two types of existence: the person who lives directly and the one whose existence is peripheral, and the damages that can be brought about when adhering too strongly to either view. The melodramatic *The Eagle with Two Heads* depicts an ideal love, so absolute in its nature as to be unable to be experienced by two real human beings. They battle forcefully against fate's interdictions and, rather than live an existence filled with compromise, they take matters into their own hands and rise above that "infernal machine" by killing themselves. *Bacchus,* Cocteau's last full-length play, brings to the stage an ancient wine-harvest myth that acts as a backdrop before which the hero can lash out at the injustice and corruption within the church.

Cocteau's novels predated and anticipated the modern antinovelists. He was an innovator in that he rejected the psychological approach developed by Balzac and Flaubert among others. He abolished conventional plot lines and climax-building, discarded picturesque, romantic, sentimental, and naturalistic tendencies—all characteristic of the novels flourishing in the 1920s and 1930s. *The Great Split,* therefore, is written in sober, restrained, poetic tones. The characters, however, are ultramodern, reflecting the deep psychological disarray of contemporary society. Cocteau's creatures are, in fact, similar to Genet's in *Our Lady of the Flowers:* identityless and formless beings who hover about a make-believe world, entities with seemingly wooden feelings and farcelike natures. In *Thomas the Impostor,* Cocteau's hero, somewhat like Gide's Lafcadio, is an adolescent who finds his inner realism incompatible with the workaday world about him. None of Cocteau's other novels, however, can match the standard of his *Children of the Game,* which will remain one of the great French works of all time. The characters in this novel are shorn of all extraneous flesh; they are not three-dimensional beings, but rather opposing instincts, each trying to destroy the other in a series of sadomasochistic rounds. The objectivity, the restraint, the extreme simplicity, and the willfully naïve language used in *Children of the Game* give it the power and mythlike grandeur of ancient Greek tragedy.

Cocteau's novels are not comparable to the works of Proust, Roger Martin du Gard, Jules Romains, or André Malraux. He was neither interested in proving a philosophical point (with perhaps the exception of *Bacchus*), nor in exploring his own psychological depths, nor even in explicating a politico-economic system. What mattered most to Cocteau was the creation of a play whose mood of mystery and magic, whose imaginative power and poetic qualities, and whose shock technique would bring about audience participation. Because his protaginists were never flesh-and-blood people, but rather symbols or embodiments of instincts, mythological beings, or states of happiness or sadness, his works created in his readers a different kind of tension than they were accustomed to at the time. They were disoriented by Cocteau's works and suffered a kind of malaise. Today, Nathalie Saurraute in *Portrait d'un inconnu* and *Martereau* inflicts a similar type of distress on her readers by inducing a fresh view from which a new world emerges. Robert Pinget's *The Inquisitory* (*L'Inquisitoire*), Michel Butor's *Milan Passage* (*Passage de Milan*) and *Degrés,* and Alain Robbe-Grillet's *The Labyrinth* and the *Peeping Tom* (*Le Voyeur*) bring a similar disturbance to the reader's psyche.

Though Cocteau's poetry was of a very high quality, it does not have the same degree of originality as his novels or plays. *The Cape of Good Hope,* in which the image of the plane is used with such dynamism and verve, is a fine period piece, as are Cocteau's antiwar poems, *Poetry.* The beautiful imagery in "Spain" in which time and space became fluid, in which concrete objects are treated in terms of their component parts, is remarkable. The tone of suffering in *Number 7* and the musicality so disturbing in *The Crucifixion* are memorable. Yet, Cocteau's poems cannot approach, for instance, the grandeur and power of Paul Claudel's visionary and apocalyptic verses and whether they will remain as permanent adornments of French poetry is perhaps questionable.

As an essayist and polemicist, Cocteau left fascinating portraits of his contemporaries: Proust, Apollinaire, Gide, Modigliani, Picasso; and of past literary figures such as Jean-Jacques Rousseau. He was ahead of his time when he championed atonal music, fighting valiantly for Stravinsky's early works, French music, and particularly the compositions of Erik Satie and "The Six." Cocteau's essays are fascinating, in that they lend insights on the great creative personalities of the period as well as on various movements and artistic trends, but they are not unique in their genre, and certainly do not have the transcendental qualities of those of Montaigne or Dryden or even Pope. They suffer from a certa... superficiality and an unwillingness, or perhaps an inability, to bore deeply within the human personality.

Cocteau was a good artist. He drew pictures of Apollinaire, Satie, Picasso, Colette, and more. His portraits can be recognized at a glance because they all bear Cocteau's personal trademark: a star, an angel, stairs. He did not, however, fall into the class of the Modiglianis or the Braques. First and foremost, Cocteau was not possessed of artistic genius. Secondly, painting and drawing were secondary considerations for him. They were an avocation rather than a vocation. Cocteau, however, was a sound and discerning art critic. His statements concerning Picasso are examples of his virtually prophetic vision. *The Indirect Method,* in which Cocteau devotes so many pages to de Chirico, is outstanding because of the stress he lays on this painter's mystical and religious outlook, the role of the "displaced" object that tells a story in itself, the symbolic overtones of the artist's pigmentations. Yet, though Cocteau's art criticisms are documents of stature, fascinating for the light they shed on the works of his contemporaries, they do not have the depth, for example of Antonin Artaud's essay on Van Gogh, a work which penetrates the very roots of this painter's art, his motivations, his use of color and tortuous lines, his confrontation with life; indeed, one of the most profound art criticisms written in the twentieth century.

Aside from Cocteau's novels and his plays, he contributed greatly to the film industry. Here he was able to combine his literary and visual talents, those he could neither fulfill in his poetry or in his drawings. *The Blood of a Poet* has all the hallmarks of a masterpiece, uniqueness of vison, and impeccable execution. *Orpheus, Beauty and the Beast, The Eagle with Two Heads,* and *Intimate Relations* are also unusual films, from both a photographic and literary point of view. Cocteau's use of closeups, the focused and restrained emotions, the extreme simplicity of gestures, the sparseness and objectivity of dialogue, and the deliberate and effective timing of sequences all contribute to memorable hours in the movie theater.

For years to come, Cocteau will be remembered as a vital and powerful force in the domain of the film, the theater, and the novel.

# Notes and References

*Chapter One*

1. *Oeuvres complètes,* vol. 11, *Potraits-souvenir* (Paris: Marguerat), 37.
2. These three volumes were later repudiated by Cocteau.
3. *Entretiens avec André Fraigneau* (Paris: Seuil, 1965), 21.
4. *Poésie critique,* vol. 1 (Paris: Gallimard, 1959), 105.
5. Ned Rorem, "Cocteau and Music," in *Cocteau and the French Scene* (New York: Abbeville Press, 1984), 155.

*Chapter Two*

1. *Oeuvres complètes,* vol. 9, *Le Coq et l'Arlequin,* 53.
2. *La Difficulté d'être* (Paris: Morihien, 1947), 32.
3. *Oeuvres complètes,* vol. 11, *Le Potomak,* 13.
4. Ibid., 111.
5. Ibid., 112.
6. *Oeuvres complètes,* vol. 9, *Le Secret professionnel,* 198.
7. *Poésie critique,* vol. 1, 217.
8. *Oeuvres complètes,* vol. 1, *Le Coq et l'Arlequin,* 40.
9. *Oeuvres complètes,* vol. 2, *Le Potomak,* 15.
10. *Oeuvres completes,* vol. 4, *Le Discours du grand sommeil,* 82.
11. Ibid., 46.
12. Ibid., 25.
13. Ibid., 82.
14. *Oeuvres complètes,* vol. 3, *Le Cap de Bonne-Espérance,* 82.
15. Dargelos, the bully in *Children of the Game,* may be an anagram for Roland Garros. Roland Garros was later taken prisoner of war in Germany.
16. Blaise Cendrars had just returned from the United States and was in need, as was Cocteau, of a publisher. For this reason they founded their own firm.
17. Roger Lannes, *Jean Cocteau* (Paris: Seghers, 1947), 30.
18. Eric Walter White, *Stravinsky* (London: John Lehman, 1947), 50.
19. *Oeuvres complètes,* vol. 9, *Le Secret professionnel,* 170.
20. Ibid., 53.
21. Ibid., 244.
22. *Poésie critique,* vol. 1, 244.
23. *Oeuvres complètes,* vol. 9, *Picasso,* 244.
24. Ibid., *Le Coq et l'Arlequin,* 31.

25. Ibid., *Picasso*, 244.

26. *Entretiens avec André Fraigneau*, 23.

27. André Gide, *Journals*, vol. 1 (Paris: Gallimard, 1951–54), 688.

28. *La Difficulte d'être*, 118.

29. *Oeuvres complètes*, vol. 9, *Le Coq et l'Arlequin*, 25. *Le Coq et l'Arlequin* was first published in Les Editions de la Sirene, which Cocteau had founded with Cendrars, and included a picture of Cocteau and two monograms by Picasso.

30. Ibid., 24.

31. *Journal d'un inconnu* (Paris: Grasset, 1953), 111.

*Chapter Three*

1. *Oeuvres complètes*, vol. 9, *Le Secret professionnel*, 188.

2. *Oeuvres complètes*, vol. 3, *Plain-Chant*, 236.

3. Ibid, *Poésies*, 138.

4. Ibid., 139.

5. Ibid., *Plain-Chant*, 238.

6. Ibid., 245.

7. *Oeuvres complètes*, vol. 9, *Le Secret professionnel*, 167.

8. 188.

9. Ibid., 177.

10. Ibid., *D'un ordre considéré comme une anarchie*, 208.

11. Michael Benedikt and George Wellwarth, *Modern French Theatre* (New York: Dutton, 1966), 95.

12. *Oeuvres complètes*, vol. 9, *Le Secret professionnel*, 216.

13. Benedikt and Wellwarth, *Modern French Theatre*, 103.

14. Ibid., 107.

15. Ibid., 108.

16. Ibid., 94.

17. *Oeuvres complètes*, vol. 9, *D'un ordre considéré comme une anarchie*, 222.

18. Ibid., *Autour de Thomas l'Imposteur*, 232.

19. *Oeuvres complètes*, vol. 1, *Le Grand écart*, 20.

20. Ibid., 35.

21. Ibid., 20.

22. Ibid., 89.

23. Ibid., 36.

24. Ibid., 79.

25. Ibid., 32.

26. Ibid., 33.

27. Ibid., 47.

28. Ibid., *Thomas l'Imposteur*, 107.

29. Ibid., 112.

30. Ibid., 143.

31. Ibid., 109.
32. Ibid., 109.
33. Ibid., 132.
34. *Thomas the Impostor,* trans. Dorothy Williams (Genève: Marguerat, 1946), 23.

## Chapter Four

1. *Oeuvres complètes,* vol. 9, *Lettre à Jacques Maritain,* 295.
2. André Fraigneau, *Cocteau par lui-même* (Paris: Seuil, 1965), 49.
3. Gide, *Journal,* vol. 1, 754.
4. *Oeuvres complètes,* vol. 9, *Lettre á Jacques Maritain,* 278.
5. *Poésie critique,* vol. 1, 211.
6. *Oeuvres complètes,* vol. 9, *Lettre à Jacques Maritain,* 278.
7. *Oeuvres complètes,* vol. 9, *Opéra,* 103.
8. Ibid., 119.
9. Ibid., 151.
10. Ibid., 152.
11. Many of these images appear in Cocteau's film scenario *The Blood of a Poet* and *The Children of the Game.*
12. *Oeuvres complètes,* vol. 9, *Opera,* 106.
13. "The Angel Heurtebise" was first published in 1925 with a photograph of Man Ray: It was later included in *Opéra,* with a cover designed by Christian Bérard.
14. *Journal d'un inconnu,* 49.
15. *Oeuvres complètes,* vol. 9, *Opéra,* 128.
16. Ibid., *Lettre à Jacques Maritain,* 303.
17. Ibid., *La jeunesse et le scandale,* 345.
18. *Cocteau: Five Plays,* trans. Carl Wildman (London: Oxford University Press, 1962), 29.
19. The same fate was suffered by Pentheus.
20. He is like Dargelos in *The Children of the Game.*
21. *Cocteau: Five Plays,* trans. Wildman, 29.
22. *Journal d'un inconnu,* 48–50.
23. Ibid., 222.
24. White, *Stravinsky,* 120.
25. *Oeuvres complètes,* vol. 10, *Opium,* 53.
26. *Oeuvres complétes,* vol. 9, *Une entrevue sur la critique,* 36.

## Chapter Five

1. *Oeuvres complètes,* vol. 10, *Le Mystere laïc,* 31.
2. *Oeuvres complètes,* vol. 7, Preface to *La Voix humaine,* 54.
3. *The Human Voice,* starring Anna Magnani, was filmed by Jean Coc-

teau and Roberto Rossellini in 1947. It was performed at the Opéra Comique in Paris with music composed by Francis Poulenc.

4. *Opium,* trans. Margaret Crosland and Sinclair Road (Geneve: Marguerat, 1950), 148.

5. *Oeuvres complètes,* vol. 1, *Les Enfants terribles,* 199.

6. *Opium,* 24.

7. Jean Genet's plays *Death Watch* and *The Maids* can be analyzed in a similar fashion.

8. *Oeuvres complètes,* vol. 2, *Les Enfants terribles,* 72.

9. Ibid., 249.

10. Ibid., 234.

11. Ibid., 282.

12. Ibid., 240.

13. Ibid., 221.

14. Ibid., 249.

15. Ibid., 202.

16. Ibid., 207.

17. Ibid., 284.

18. Cocteau prepared the scenario and dialogue for the film *Children of the Game* (1950). He also spoke the commentaries. The background music of Bach and Vivaldi perfectly suited the restrained and classic tempo of the film.

19. Fraigneau, *Cocteau,* 61.

20. *Professional Secrets,* trans. Richard Howard (New York: Farrar, Straus & Giroux, 1970), 147.

21. *Entretiens avec André Fraigneau,* 90.

22. Rorem, "Cocteau and Music," 169.

23. *The Infernal Machine and Other Plays by Jean Cocteau,* trans. Albert Bermel (New York: New Directions Books, 1963), 6.

24. Francis Fergusson, *The Idea of a Theatre* (Princeton: Princeton University Press, 1949), 209–12.

25. *The Infernal Machine and Other Plays by Jean Cocteau,* trans. Albert Bermel, 6.

26. Ibid., 25.

27. *Oeuvres complètes,* vol. 5, *La Machine infernale,* 227.

28. *The Infernal Machine and Other Plays by Jean Cocteau,* trans. Albert Bermel, 58.

29. *Oeuvres complètes,* vol. 5, *La Machine infernale,* 227.

30. *The Infernal Machine and Other Plays by Jean Cocteau,* trans. Albert Bermel, 58.

31. Ibid., 94.

32. Ibid., vol. 10, *Le mystère laïc,* 20.

33. Ibid., *Essai de critique indirecte,* 197.

34. Ibid., *Le mystère laïc,* 31.

35. Ibid., 46.
36. *Entretiens avec André Fraigneau*, 99.
37. *Oeuvres complètes*, vol. 6, *Les Chevaliers de la Table ronde*, 120.
38. C. G. Jung, *Psychological Types*, 290.
39. *The Knights of the Round Table*, trans. W. H. Auden (New York: New Directions Books, 1963), 284.

*Chapter Six*

1. *Oeuvres complètes*, vol. 2, *Fin du Potomak*, 192.
2. *Oevures complètes*, vol. 7, *Les Parents terribles*, 84.
3. Milorad, "Un enfant terrible écrit *Les Parents terribles*," *Cahiers Jean Cocteau*, vol. 5, (Paris: Gallimard, 1969–79), 57.
4. *Oeuvres complètes*, vol. 7, *Les Parents terribles*, 230.
5. Such an outcome in a Cocteau play is not surprising since Michel is, in effect, a projection of the author-poet, who cannot bear to see himself dead when his "beautiful life" is just unfolding.
6. *Oeuvres complètes*, vol. 7, *Les Parents terribles*, 83.
7. *Oeuvres complètes*, vol. 2, *La Fin du Potomak*, 202.
8. Ibid., 214.
9. Ibid., 232.
10. Ibid., 192.
11. *Oeuvres complètes*, vol. 8, *Les Monstres sacrés*, 199.
12. *Cocteau: Five Plays*, trans. Edward O. Marsh (London: MacGibbon & Kee, 1962), 216.
13. Ibid., 193.
14. Ibid., 194.
15. *Oeuvres complètes*, vol. 8, *La Machine à écrire*.
16. *Oeuvres complètes*, vol. 10, *Le Mythe du Greco*, 306.
17. *Beauty and the Beast*, trans. Robert Hammond (New York: New York University Press, 1970), 77.

*Chapter Seven*

1. *Poésie critique*, vol. 2, "Lettre aux Américains".
2. Fraigneau, *Cocteau*, 91.
3. *Entretiens avec André Fraigneau*, 140.
4. *The Eagle with Two Heads* was made into a film in 1948 and starred Jean Marais and Edwige Feuillere.
5. *Entretiens avec André Fraigneau*, 139.
6. *Cocteau: Five Plays*, trans. Carl Wildman, 301.
7. Ibid., 310.
8. Ibid., 304.
9. Ibid., 251.

10. Ibid., 306.

11. Ibid., 266.

11. Ibid., 299.

13. Ibid., 267.

14. Ibid., 279.

15. Ibid., 282.

16. Jean Cocteau also supervised the filming of *Ruy Blas* by Victor Hugo.

17. Fraigneauy, *Cocteau*, 100.

18. *Poésie critique*, vol. 2, "Lettre aux Américains".

19. Ibid.

20. Fraigneau, *Cocteau*, 109.

21. *Bacchus* (Paris: Gallimard, 1952), 218.

22. Ibid., 70.

23. Ibid., 51.

24. Ibid., 119.

25. Ibid., 125.

26. Ibid., 131.

27. Ibid., 192.

28. Ibid., 152.

29. Ibid., 200.

30. Ibid., 53.

31. *Journal d'un inconnu*, 171.

32. Ibid., 188.

33. Cocteau pursued this same vein in *Discours sur la poésie*, a speech given at the International Fair in Brussels on 19 September 1958. He confessed the difficult road that lies ahead for anyone who takes poetic art seriously—no matter what its form. Poetry is not a pleasure—it is a catastrophe, as is any great gift.

34. *Poésie critique*, vol. 2, *Le Discours d'Oxford* (Paris: Gallimard, 1959), 195.

35. *Appogiatures* (Monaco: Ed. du Rocher, 1953), 9.

# Selected Bibliography

PRIMARY SOURCES

*Performing Arts*

*Orphée.* Genève: Marguerat, 1948. *Orpheus.* Translated by Carl Wildman. London: Oxford University Press, 1962. Translated by John Savacool in *The Infernal Machine and Other Plays.* New York: New Directions Books, 1963.

*Oedipe-Roi.* Genève; Marguerat, 1948.

*Antigone.* Genève: Marguerat, 1948. *Antigone.* Translated by Carl Wildman. London: Oxford University Press. London: MacGibbon & Kee, 1962.

*La Machine infernale. The Infernal Machine.* Translated by Carl Wildman. London: Oxford University Press, 1936. *The Infernal Machine and Other Plays.* Translated by Albert Bermel. New York: New Directions Books, 1963.

*Les Chevaliers de la Table Ronde.* Genève: Marguerat, 1948. *The Knights of the Round Table.* Translated by W. H. Auden. New York: New Directions Books, 1963.

*Renaud et Armide.* Genève: Marguerat, 1948.

*Les Mariés de la Tour Eiffel.* Genève: Marguerat, 1948. *The Wedding on the Eiffel Tower.* Translated by Michael Benedikt in *Modern French Plays.* London: Faber & Faber, 1964. *The Eiffel Tower Wedding Party.* Translated by Dudley Fitts. In *The Infernal Machine and Other Plays.* New York: New Directions Books, 1963.

*La Voix humaine.* Genève: Marguerat, 1948. *The Human Voice* Translated by Carl Wildman. London: Vision Press, 1951.

*Les Parents terribles.* Genève: Marguerat, 1948. *Intimate Relations.* Translated by Charles Frank. London: MacGibbon & Kee, 1962.

*Parade.* Genève: Marguerat, 1948.

*Le Boeuf sur le toit.* Genève: Marguerat, 1948.

*La Machine à écrire.* Genève: Marguerat, 1949. *The Typewriter.* Translated by Ronald Duncan. London: Dennis Dobson, 1947.

*Les Monstres sacrés.* Genève: Marguerat, 1949. *The Holy Terrors.* Translated by Edward O. Marsh. London: MacGibbon & Kee, 1962. *The Holy Terrors.* Translated by Rosamond Lehman. New York: New Directions Books, 1957.

*L'Aigle à deux têtes.* Paris: Gallimard, 1946. *The Eagle Has Two Heads.* Adapted

by Ronald Duncan. London: Vision Press, 1948. *The Eagle With Two Heads*. Translated by Carl Wildman. London: MacGibbon & Kee, 1962.
*Bacchus*. Paris: Gallimard, 1952. *Bacchus* Translated by Mary C. Hoeck in *The Infernal Machine and Other Plays*. New York: New Directions Books, 1963.

### Novels

*Le Grand écart*. Genève: Marguerat, 1946. *The Great Split*. Translated by Lewis Galantiere. London: Putnam, 1925.
*Thomas l'Imposteur*. Genève: Marguerat, 1946. *The Imposter*. Translated by Lewis Galantiere. New York: Appleton, 1925. *The Imposter*. Translated by Dorothy Williams. London: Peter Owen, 1957.
*Les Enfants terribles*. Genève: Marguerat, 1946. *Enfants terribles*. Translated by Samuel Putnam. New York: Brewer & Warren, 1930. *The Children of the Game*. Translated by Rosamond Lehmann. London: Harvill Press, 1955.

### Collections of Prose, Poetry, Essays, Letters

*Le Potomak, La Fin du Potomak*. Genève: Marguerat, 1947.
*Le Rappel à l'ordre*. Genève: Marguerat, 1950. *A Call to Order*. Translated by Rollo H. Myers. London: Faber & Gwyer, 1926.
*Le Cap de Bonne-Espérance, Poésies, Plain-chant*. Genève: Marguerat, 1947.
*Discours du grand sommeil, Opéra, Léone, La Crucifixion*. Genève: Marguerat, 1947.
*Clair-Obscur*. Monaco: Rocher, 1954.
*Le Mystere laïc, Des beaux-arts considérés comme un assassinat, Quelques articles, Préfaces, Le mythe du Greco, Coupoures de presse*. Genève: Marguerat, 1950.
*Opium*. Genève: Marguerat, 1950. Translated by Ernest Boyd. London: Longmans, 1932. Translated by Margaret Crossland and Sinclair Road. London: Peter Owen, 1957. New York: Grove Press, 1958.
*Portraits-souvenir, Mon premier voyage, Le foyer des artistes*. Genève: Marguerat, 1951.
*Le Livre blanc*. Paris: Quatre-chemins, 1928. Paris: Olympia Press, 1957.
*La Difficulté d'être*. Paris: Morihien, 1947. Translated by Elizabeth Sprigge. London: Peter Owen, 1966. New York: Coward McCann, 1967.
*Journal d'un inconnu*. Paris: Grasset, 1953. *Past Tense. Diaries*. Vol. 1., Translated by Richard Howard. New York; Harcourt Brace Jovanovitch, 1987.

### Film Scripts

*Le Sang d'un poète* (music by Auric), 1932. Translated by Lily Pons. New York: Bodley Press, 1949.
*Le Baron fantôme* (dialogue by Cocteau), 1943.

*L'Eternel retour* (music by Auric, scenario and dialogue by Cocteau), 1944.
*La Belle et la bête* (music by Auric), 1945. Translated by Robert Hammond. New York: New York University Press, 1970. *Diary of a Film. La Belle et la Bête*. Translated by Ronald Duncan. London: Dobson, 1950. New York: Roy, 1950.
*Ruy Blas* (adaptation by Cocteau), 1947.
*Les Parents terribles* (music by Auric), 1948.
*L'Aigle à deux têtes* (music by Auric), 1948.
*Orphée* (music by Auric), 1950.
*Les Enfants terribles* (scenario and dialogue by Cocteau), 1950.
*Le Testament d'Orphée*, 1960.
*Two Screenplays*. Translated by Carol Martin-Sperry. New York: Orion Press, 1968.
*Three Screenplays*. Translated by Carol Martin-Sperry. New York: Grossman Publishers, 1972.

## SECONDARY SOURCES

*Books*

Brosse, Jacques. *Cocteau*. Paris: Gallimard, 1970. Good study.
Brown, Frederick. *An Impersonation of Angels*. New York: Viking Press, 1968. Emphasis on the times rather than on the works.
*Cahiers Jean Cocteau*. Vols. 1–8. Paris: Gallimard, 1969–79. Rather superficial approach to Cocteau and his writings.
Crosland, Margaret. *Cocteau*. New York: Alfred A. Knopf, 1956. Excellent study of Cocteau's works.
Dubourg, Pierre. *La Dramaturgie de Jean Cocteau*. Paris: Grasset, 1954. Interesting insights on Cocteau's theater.
Evans, Arthur B. *Jean Cocteau and His Orphic Identity*. Philadelphia: Art Alliance Press, 1977. A penetrating study of some of Cocteau's works.
Fermigier, Andre. *Jean Cocteau entre Picasso et Radiguet*. Paris: Hermann, 1967. Insights into Cocteau's friendships with other artists.
Fowlie, Wallace. *Jean Cocteau*. Bloomington: Indiana University Press, 1966. A basic book on Cocteau.
Fraigneau, André. *Cocteau par lui-même*. Paris: Seuil, 1965. An enjoyable biography of Cocteau.
Jacob, Max. *Lettres à Jean Cocteau: 1919–1944*. Paris: Morihien, 1950. These letters shed light on Cocteau's intellectual and emotional development.
Jung, C. G. *Symbols of Transformation*. New York: Pantheon, 1956.
———. *The Archetypes and the Collective Unconscious*. New York: Pantheon,

1959. These psychological studies help better understand Cocteau, the man, and his works.

Lannes, Roger. *Jean Cocteau*. Paris: Seghers, 1947. An easy-reading biography of Cocteau up to the year 1947.

Mauriac, Claude. *Jean Cocteau ou la vérité du mensonge*. Paris: O.C.O., 1956. A one-sided and rambling approach to Cocteau and his works.

Mourgue, Gérard. *Jean Cocteau*. Paris: Ed. Universitaires, 1965. A rather superficial study of Cocteau's works.

Oxenhandler, Neal. *Scandal and Parade: The Theatre of Jean Cocteau*. New Jersey: Rutgers University Press, 1957. An excellent study of Cocteau's theatre.

Rorem, Ned. "Cocteau and Music." In *Cocteau and the French Scene*. New York: Abbeville Press, 1984. Interesting views on Cocteau's musical affinities.

Steegmuller, Francis. *Cocteau: A Biography*. Boston: Little, Brown & Co., 1970. Excellent study.

*Journal*

Beylie, Claude. *L'Avant Scène du Cinema*. Vol. 56. February 1966. Highly interesting special issue devoted to Cocteau.

*Works with Chapters on Cocteau*

Benedikt, Michael, and George Wellworth. *Modern French Theatre*. New York: Dutton, 1966.

Bentley, Eric. *In Search of Theater*. New York: Vintage Books, 1953. Early appraisals of Cocteau's theatrical ventures are intriguing.

Grossvogel, David. *Twentieth-Century French Drama*. New York: Columbia University Press, 1961. A fine study of certain aspects of Cocteau's theater.

Guicharnaud, Jacques. *Modern French Theater*. New Haven: Yale University Press, 1961. A good overview of Cocteau's theater.

Keller, Marjorie. *The Untutored Eye*. Rutherford: Associated University Presses, 1986. Good study on Cocteau's films.

White, Eric Walter. *Stravinsky*. London: John Lehman, 1947. Excellent study on Stravinsky with some insights into his attitude toward Cocteau.

# Index

Apollinaire, Guillaume, x, 8, 24, 25, 29, 30, 31, 42, 43
Artaud, Antonin, 53
Auric, Georges, 6, 40–41, 53, 79

Barrès, Maurice, 5, 13–14, 16
Barthet, Madame, 3
Baudelaire, 15, 24
Bérard, Christian, 10, 70, 85, 106
Bernhardt, Sarah, 2, 69, 104, 111
Bernouard, François, 5
Blanche, Jacques Emile, 6
Boccioni, Umberto, 25
Bourdet, Edouard, 79
Bourget, Paul, 17
Braque, x, 30, 32, 36, 123
Breton, André, 63
Brown, Al, 10, 94

Camus, Albert, 110–11
Casimir-Périer, Claude, 4
Catulle-Mendès, 5
Cendrars, Blaise, 8, 20, 24, 25, 32
Chagall, 30
Chaplin, Charlie, 28, 78
Chirico, 36, 86–88
Claudel, Paul, 7, 68
Cocteau, Eugénie Lecomte (mother), 1–5
Cocteau, Georges (father), 1–5
Cocteau, Jean: appearance, ix, 1; education, 3–5; death, 11–12; faith, 9; family, 1–5; founds review Schéhérazade, 5; homosexuality, 34; impact on later writers, 137–42; military service, 6–7; opium use, 4, 9, 53, 55–60, 67, 70

WORKS: PERFORMING ARTS
L'Aigle a deux têtes (The Eagle Has Two Heads), ix, 11, 111–17, 120
Antigone, 10, 53–54

Bacchus, 11, 124–30
Le Boeuf sur le toit (The Do-Nothing Bar), 9, 40–42
Les Chevaliers de la Table Ronde (The Knights of the Round Table), 10, 88–93
Le Coq et l'arlequin (The Rooster and the Harlequin), 31–33, 66
La Machine à écrire (The Typewriter), x, 11, 104–6
La Machine infernale (The Infernal Machine), x, 10, 79–86
Les Mariés de la Tour Eiffel (The Wedding on the Eiffel Tower), xi, 42–45, 80
Les Monstres sacrés (The Holy Terrors), 100–104
Oedipe-Roi (Oedipus the King), 9, 10, 55, 66–67
Orphée (Orpheus), 9, 10, 60–66, 80
Parade, 8, 26–31, 132
Les Parents Terribles (Intimate Relations), 10–11, 94–98, 120
Renaud et Armide (Renaud and Armide), 11, 106–9
La Voix humaine (The Human Voice), 69–70

NOVELS
Les Enfants terribles (The Children of the Game), x, 4, 9, 70–77
Le Grand écart (The Great Split), 9, 45–48, 62
Thomas l'Imposteur (The Imposter), x, 6, 45, 48–52, 62, 77, 132

COLLECTIONS OF PROSE, POETRY, ESSAYS, LETTERS
Le Cap de Bonne-Espérance (The Cape of Good Hope), 7, 9, 20–23, 24, 25, 35, 106
Clair-Obscur (Clear-Obscure), 11

*La Difficulté d'être (The Difficulty of Being)*, 117–19

*Discours du grand sommeil (The Discourse of the Great Sleep)*, 18–20, 24, 26, 40, 63

*La Fin du Potomak,* 98–100

*Journal d'un inconnu (Journal of One Unknown)*, 126, 130–32

*La Lampe d'Aladdin (Aladdin's Lamp)*, 4, 24

*Le Mystère laïc (Lay Mystery)*, 86–88

*Opéra,* 55–60, 77

*Opium,* 9, 67–68, 77, 123

*Plain-chant (Plain-Song)*, 35, 38–39

*Poésies,* 35–39

*Portraits-souvenir,* 2, 10, 39, 92–93

*Le Potomak,* 6, 14–18, 24, 35, 67, 123

*Le prince frivole (Frivolous Prince)*, 4, 24

*Vocabulaire (Vocabulary)*, 23–26

FILM SCRIPTS

*L'Aigle a deux têtes (The Eagle Has Two Heads)*, 121–22, 142

*La Belle et la bête (Beauty and the Beast)*, 11, 108, 142

*L'Eternel retour,* 108

*Orphée (Orpheus)*, 11, 120

*Les Parents terribles (Intimate Relations)*, 142

*Le Sang d'un poète (Blood of a Poet)*, x, 4, 10, 77–79, 142

*Le Testament d'Orphée (Orpheus' Testament)*, 121, 142

Cocteau, Marthe (sister), 1

Cocteau, Paul (brother), 1

Colette, 3

Comédie-Française, 2, 4

Daudet, Lucien, 5, 13

Daumier, 16

Debussy, Claude, 6, 8, 32

Delacroix, 2

Delaunay, 36

de Max, Edouard, 3, 4–5, 69

de Noailles, Countess Anna, 5, 13, 28

Dermit, Edouard, 11

Diaghilev, x, 6, 9, 13, 26–31, 67

Dufy, Raoul, 9, 16, 30, 40–42

Dujardin, Edouard, 16

Durey, Louis, 6

*Figaro* (newspaper), 10, 92

Fokine, 26

Footit and Chocolat, 3

Fournier, Alain, 4

France, Anatole, 17

Fratellini, 41

Galbois, Guy, ix

Garros, Roland, 7, 20, 60

Genet, Jean, 11, 108

Ghéon, Henri, 5, 13, 59

Gide, André, 5, 16, 17, 30, 32, 37, 54, 77

Giraudoux, 80

Guilbert, Yvette, 3

Hahn, Raynaldo, 5, 26

Henrion, Charles, 9, 55–60

Honegger, Arthur, 6, 53, 106

Hugo, Victor, 37

Ingres, 2

Jacob, Max, 8, 24, 25, 32

James, William, 16

Jammes, 68

Jarry, Alfred, 16, 24, 42

Klemperer, Otto, 67

la belle Otéro, 3, 104

Lautréamont, 24

Léger, 36

Lemaître, Jules, 5

Mallarmé, 23

Marais, Jean, 10, 94, 105, 111

Maritain, Jacques, x, 9, 55–60, 68

Massine, Leonide, 28, 29

Matisse, 16, 30

Mauriac, François, 4, 95, 129–30

Menotti, Gian-Carlo, 11

Milhaud, Darius, 6, 9, 40–42
Mistinguett, 3
Modigliani, Amedeo, 7, 142
Mounet-Sully, 2–3, 69
Musset, Alfred de, 19
Mussorgsky, 32

Nijinsky, 6, 13, 27–31, 118
*Nouvelle Revue Française,* 5

*Paris-Soir,* 10
Piaf, Edith, 11, 103
Picasso, x, 7–8, 25, 26–31, 32, 36, 37, 53, 86, 123
Pirandello, 54
Polaire, 3
Poulenc, Francis, 6, 32, 53
Proust, Marcel, 5, 17

Radiguet, Raymond, x, 8–9, 33, 34–52, 53, 60, 64, 119
Ravel, Maurice, 6
Réjane, Madame, 2
Reverdy, Pierre, 8, 33, 59
Rilke, Rainer Maria, 5, 24
Rimbaud, 15, 40
Rocher, René, 4
Rodin, Auguste, 5
Rolland, Romain, 17
Rorem, Ned, 8, 79
Rostand, Edmond, 5, 13

Rostand, Maurice, 5
Rubenstein, Arthur, 40

Salmon, André, 8
Sarasate, 2
Sardou, Victorien; his *Madame Sans-Gêne,* 2
Sartre, Jean-Paul, x, 110–11
Satie, Erik, 8, 26–31
"Six, The." *See* "The Six"
Stradivarius, 2, 14, 50
Stravinsky, ix, x, 6, 8, 9, 13, 17–18, 26–31, 32

Tailhade, Laurent, 5
Taillefer, Germaine, 6, 32
"The Six," 6, 8, 26, 32 40–42, 43; *see also* Auric, Georges; Honegger, Arthur; Milhaud, Darius; Poulenc, Francis; Taillefer, Germaine; Durey, Louis
Toulouse-Lautrec, 3, 16
Tzara, Tristan, 25

Verne, Jules, 10, 50, 93
Villefranche-sur-Mer, ix
Vines, Ricardo, 26
Voltaire, 49

Wagner, 8, 32
Wells, H. G., 99